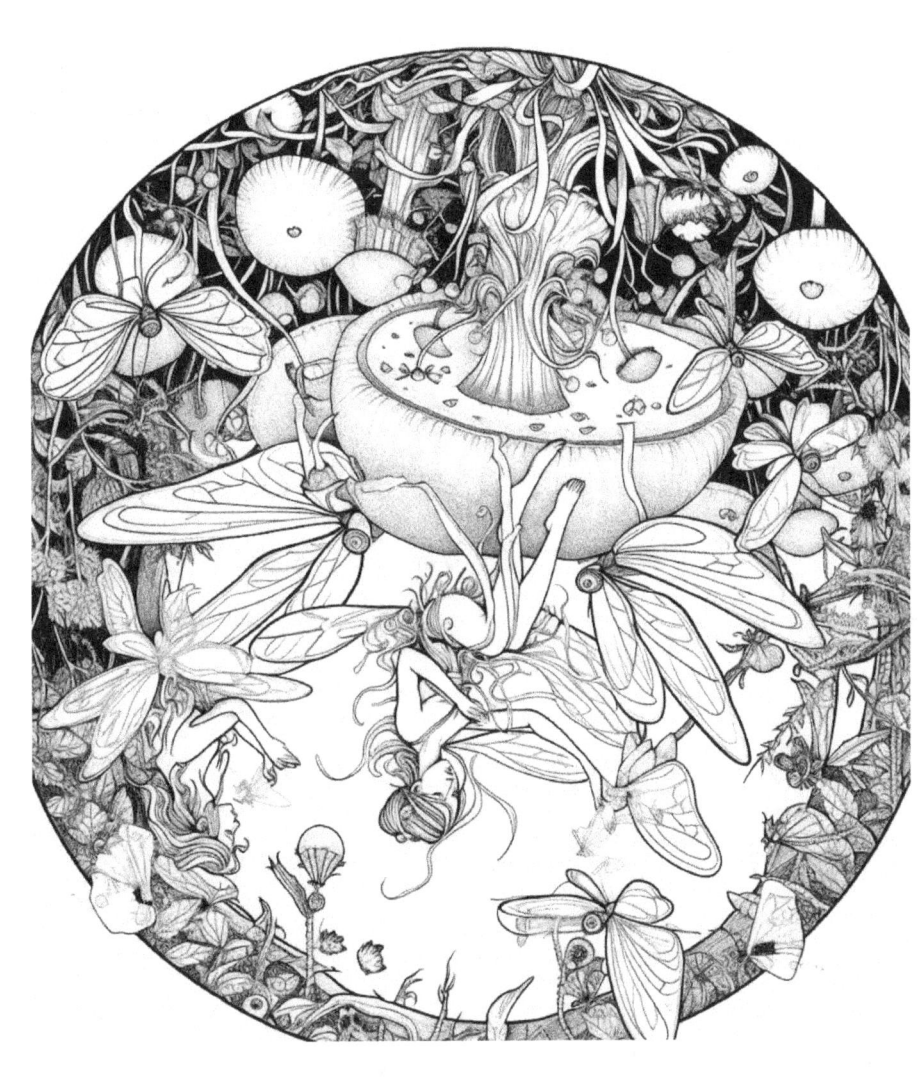

This book belongs to:

Thank you so much for choosing our coloring book!

We wanted to take a moment to express our gratitude for choosing the Fairy Landscapes adult fantasy coloring book.

It means so much to us that you have chosen to support our work, and we hope that the book brings you hours of joy and relaxation.

Creating these images was a labor of love for our team, and we are thrilled to know that they have found a home with you.

We truly believe that coloring is a wonderful way to unwind and de-stress, and we hope that you find that to be true as well.

Once again, thank you for your support. It is truly appreciated.

Enchanting Escapes Team

About Fairy Landscapes

Fairy Landscapes are a popular theme in fantasy art, often depicted as lush and magical forests, crystal clear lakes, and shimmering waterfalls. These landscapes are populated with mystical creatures, such as fairies, unicorns, and dragons, and are filled with sparkling jewels, glittering flowers, and glowing mushrooms.

Coloring pictures of this detailed coloring book for adults is a wonderful way to explore these magical worlds, to escape into a realm of fantasy and creativity, and to connect with the childlike wonder that lies within us all.

Coloring pictures of Fairy Landscapes can also be a form of self-care, as it allows you to take time out of your busy life to engage in a relaxing and enjoyable activity. It is a wonderful way to unwind after a long day, connect with your inner child, and experience a sense of playfulness and joy.

Whether you are a beginner or an experienced artist, this fairy coloring book for adults can bring you a sense of fulfillment and satisfaction, as you watch the magical worlds you create come to life on the page.

About Coloring

Whether you're new to coloring or an experienced artist, you can use a variety of tools to add color to these pages, such as colored pencils, crayons, pastels, or colored markers.

Don't be afraid to experiment with different shading techniques and textures to create your own unique style.

To ensure that your artwork looks its best, we recommend placing a blank piece of paper under the page you're working on.

This will not only protect the pages behind it but also make a handy bookmark so you can easily find your spot when you're ready to color again.

About Your new Book

Welcome to your new mystical coloring book for adults. "Fairy Landscapes"! This book is inspired by the enchanting world of fairies and their magical landscapes, featuring intricate illustrations that invite you to explore a world of fantasy and wonder.

We believe that coloring is not just for children, but can be a great way for adults to unwind and destress. Coloring in these beautiful fairy landscapes can help you relax and escape from the stresses of everyday life, allowing you to focus on the present moment and find inner peace.

We hope that this fantasy coloring book will inspire you to rediscover your creativity and imagination, while also providing a calming and meditative experience.

So grab your favorite coloring tools and let your inner artist take flight in the magical world of "Fairy Landscapes"!

If you enjoy this book, please let us and others know by leaving a review on Amazon :-)

Fairies left this blank for you

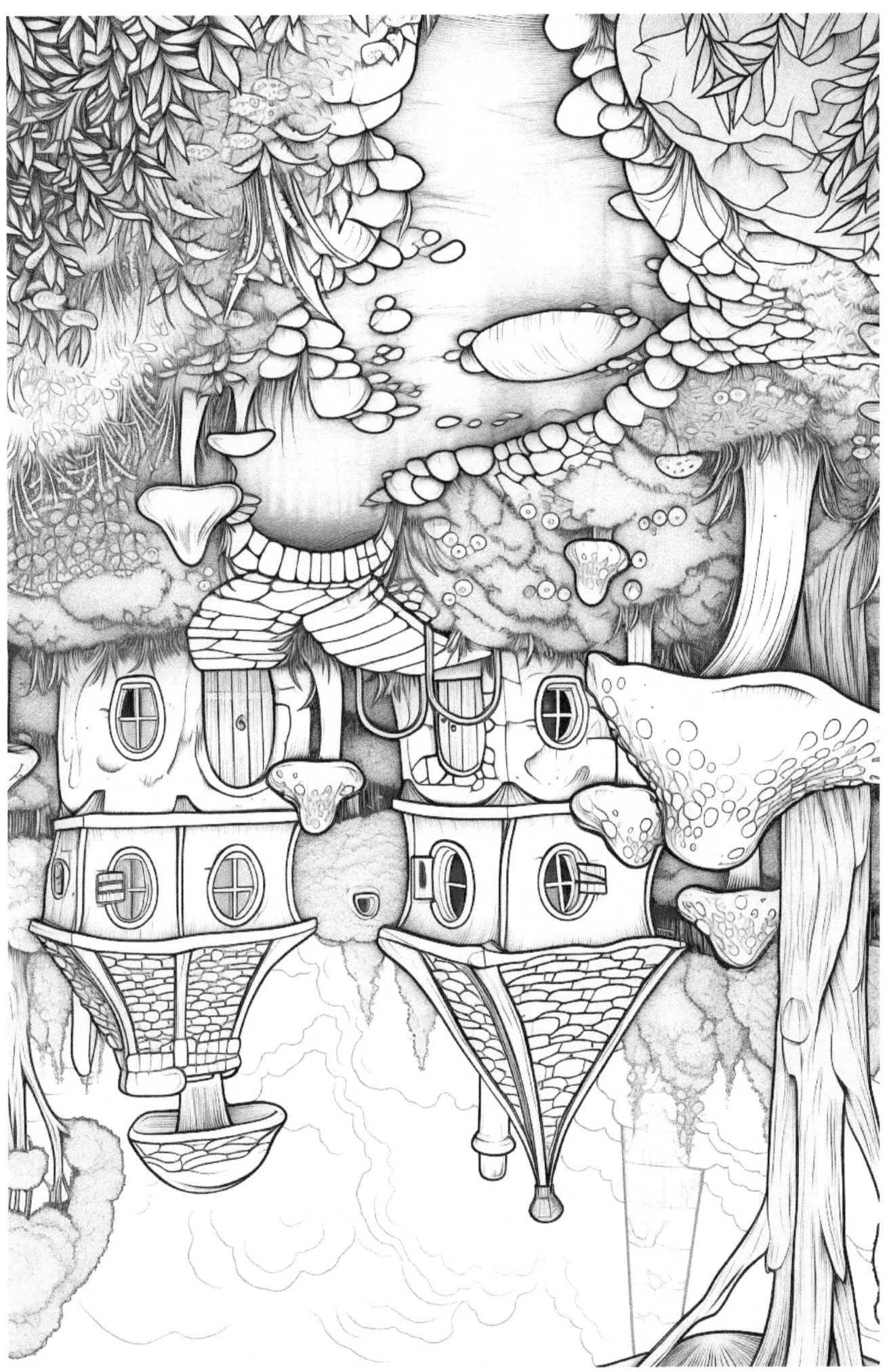

Fairies left this blank for you

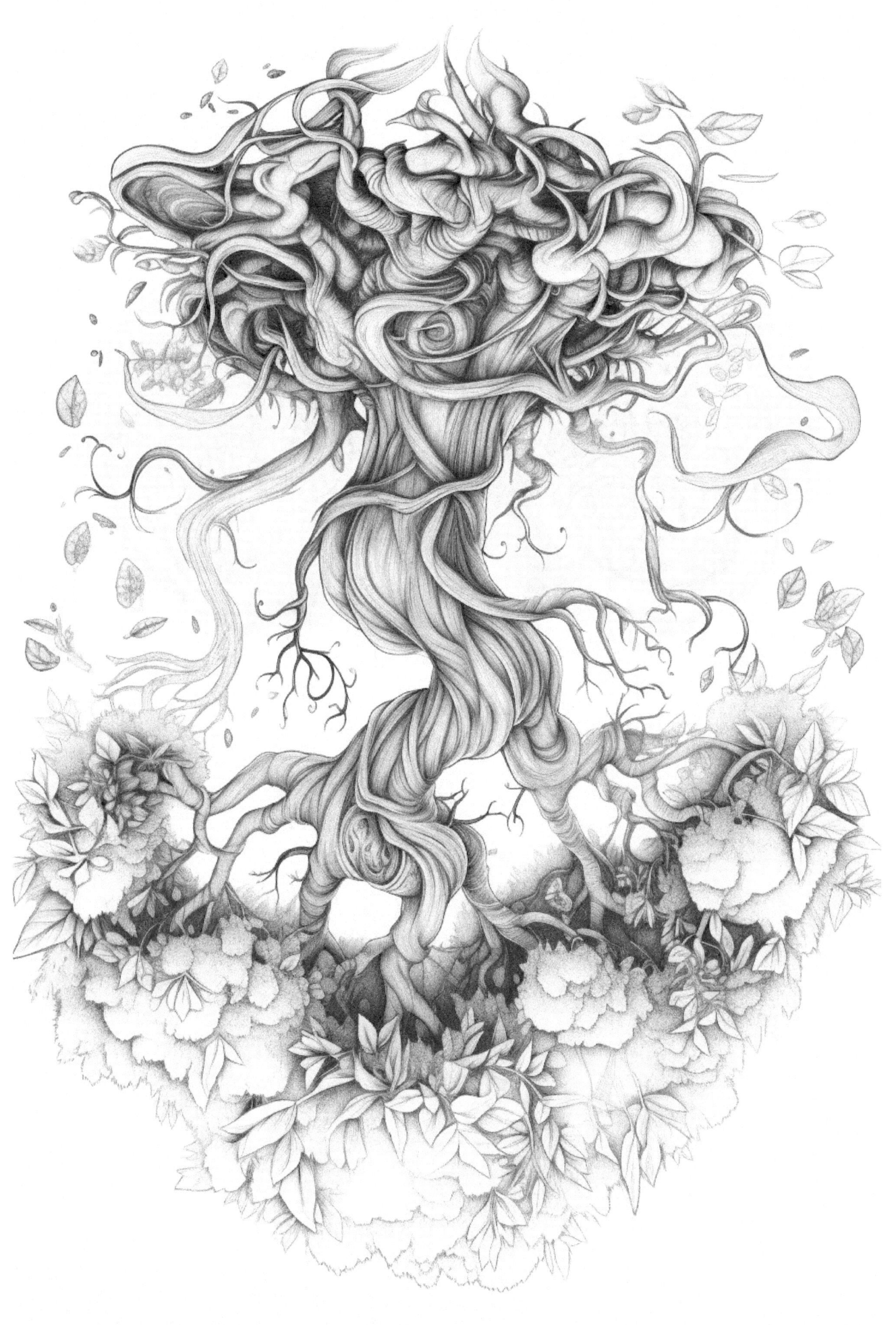

Fairies left this blank for you

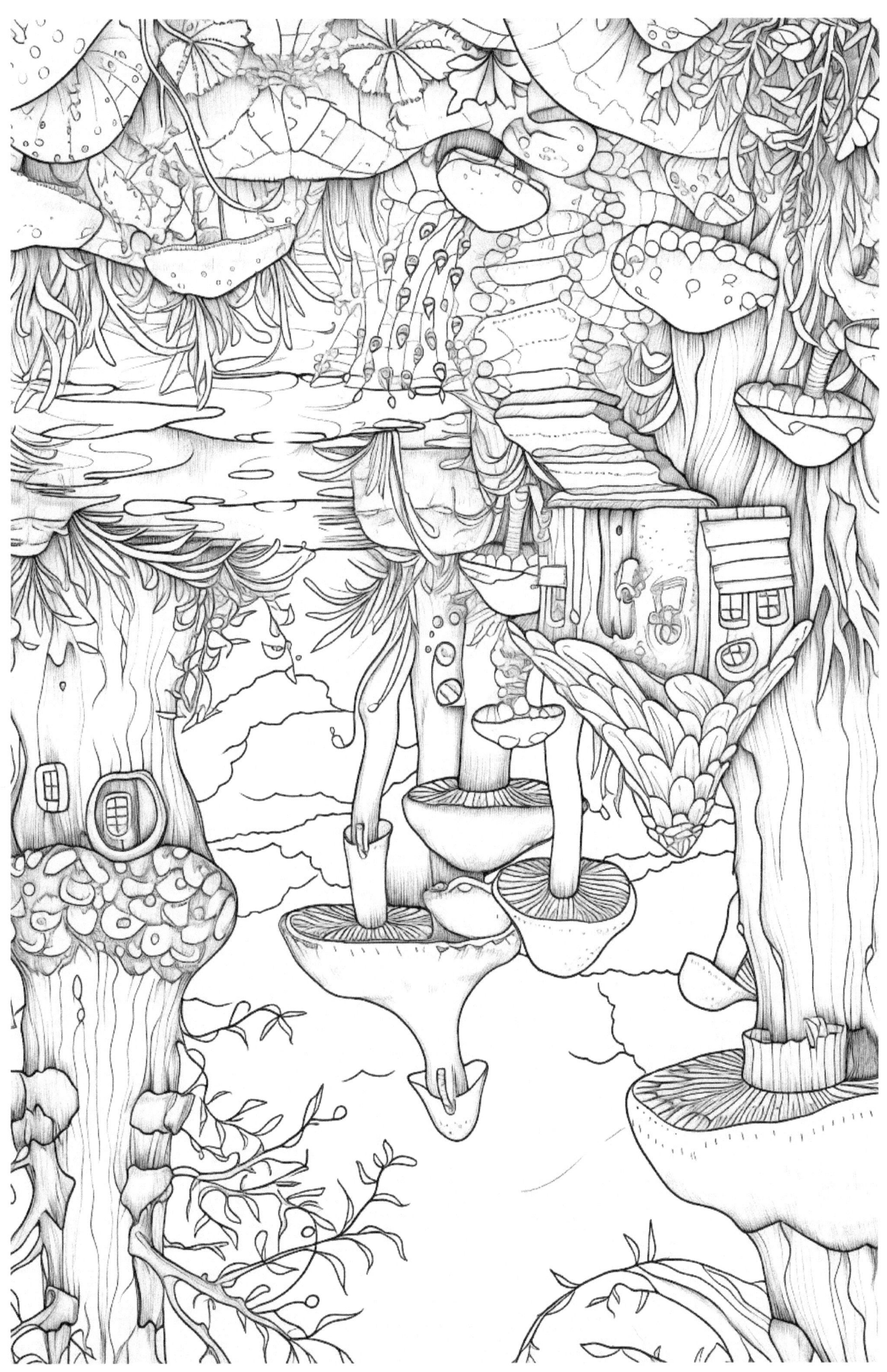

Fairies left this blank for you

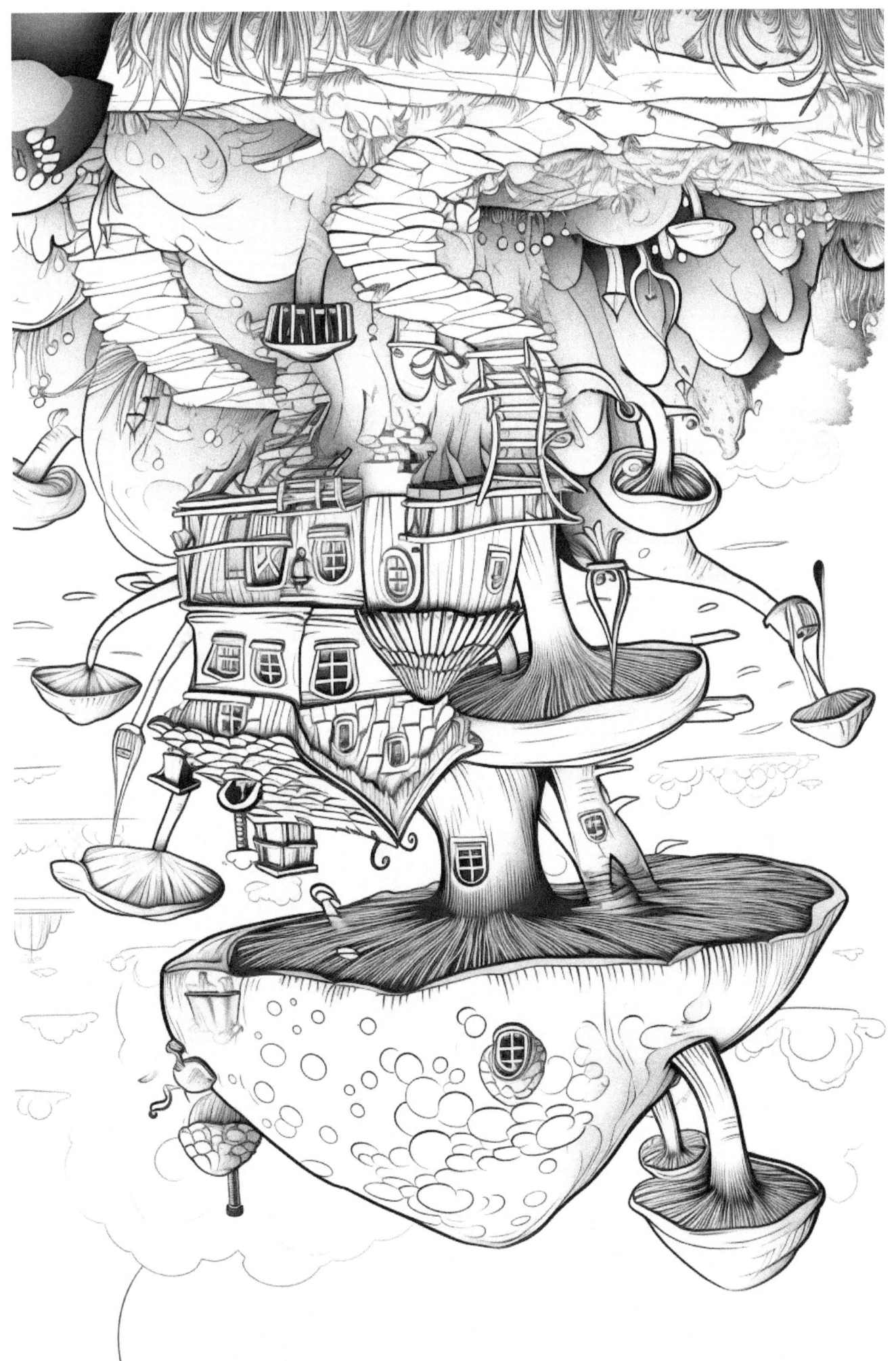

Fairies left this blank for you

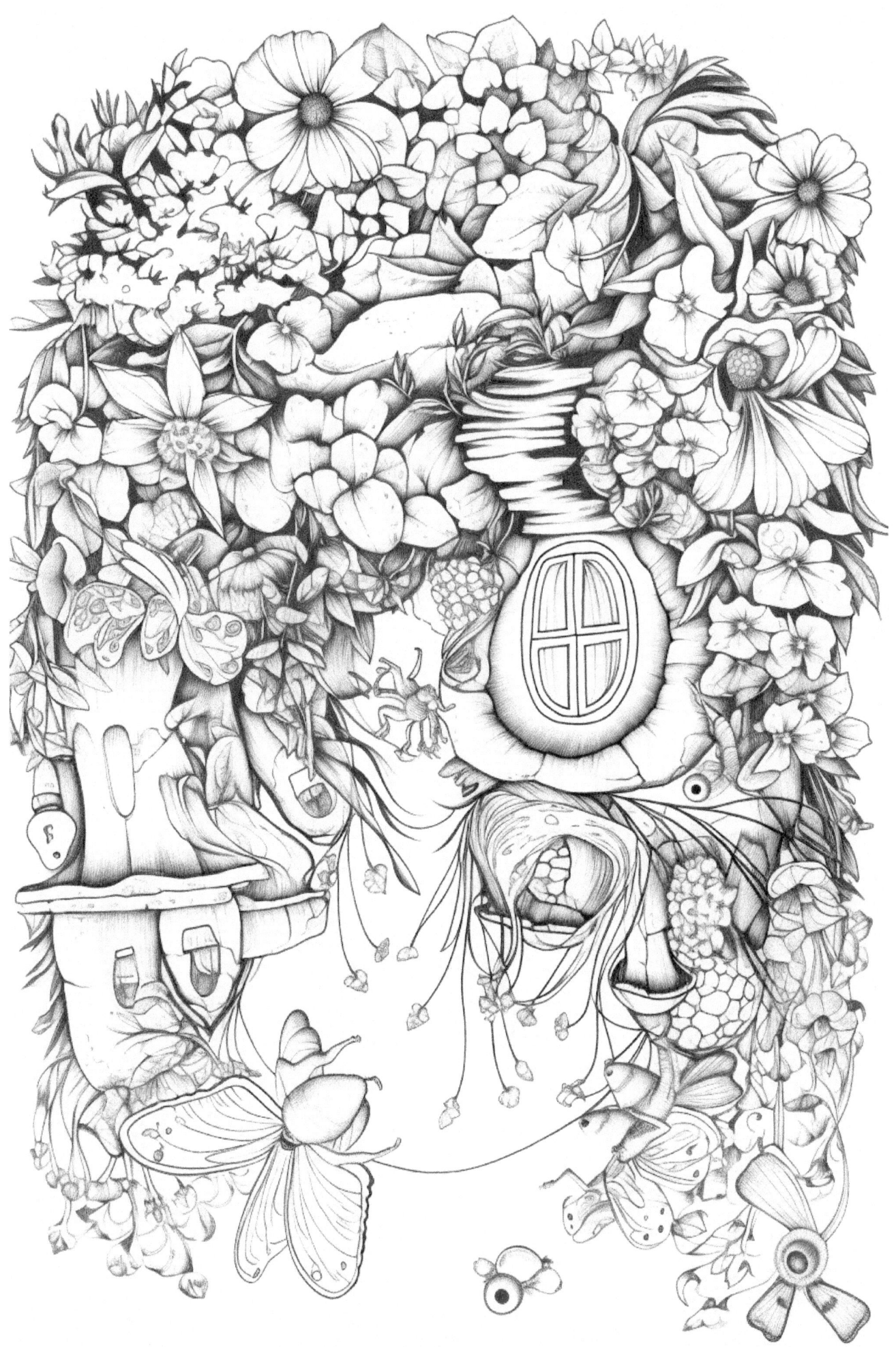

Fairies left this blank for you

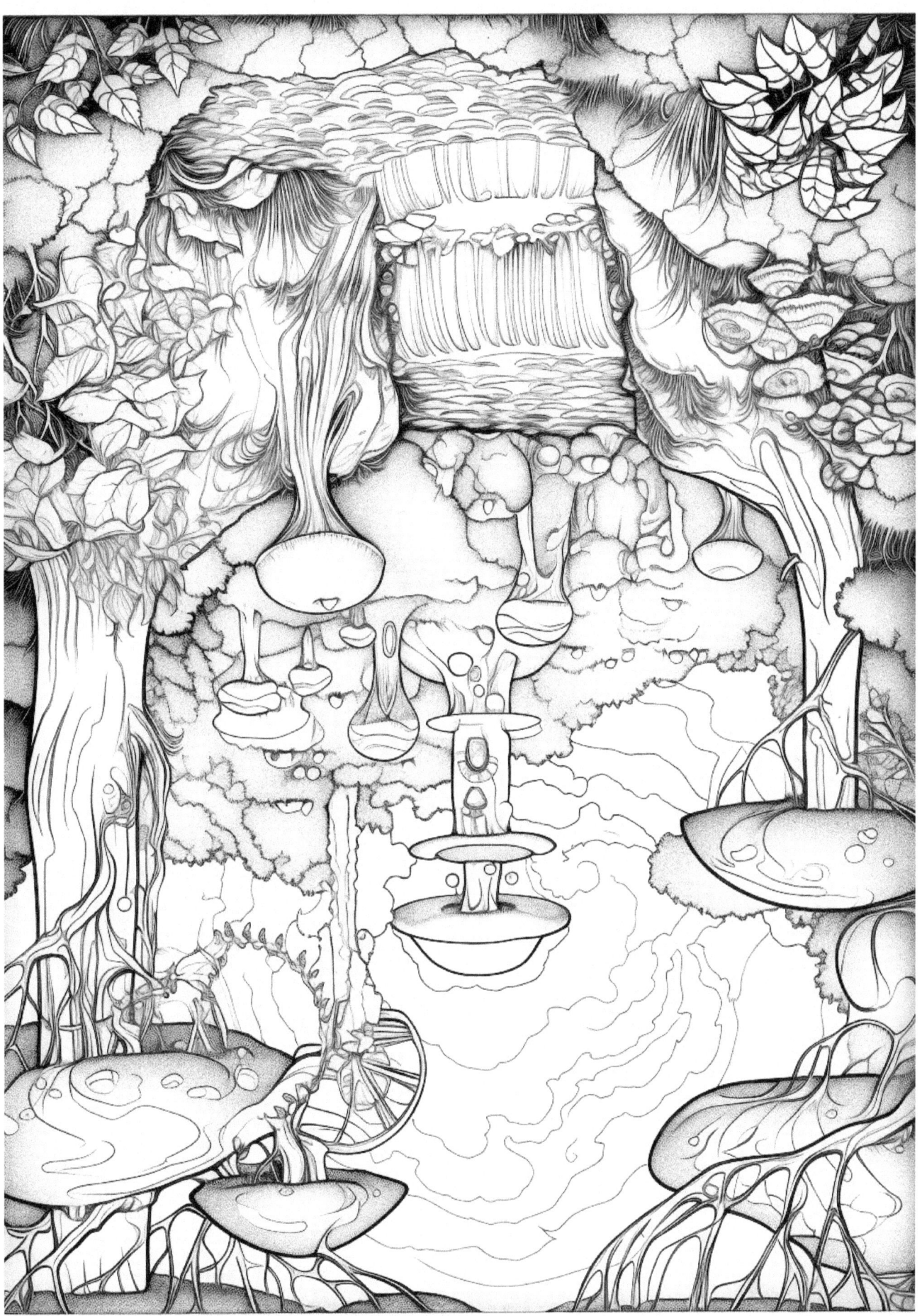

Fairies left this blank for you

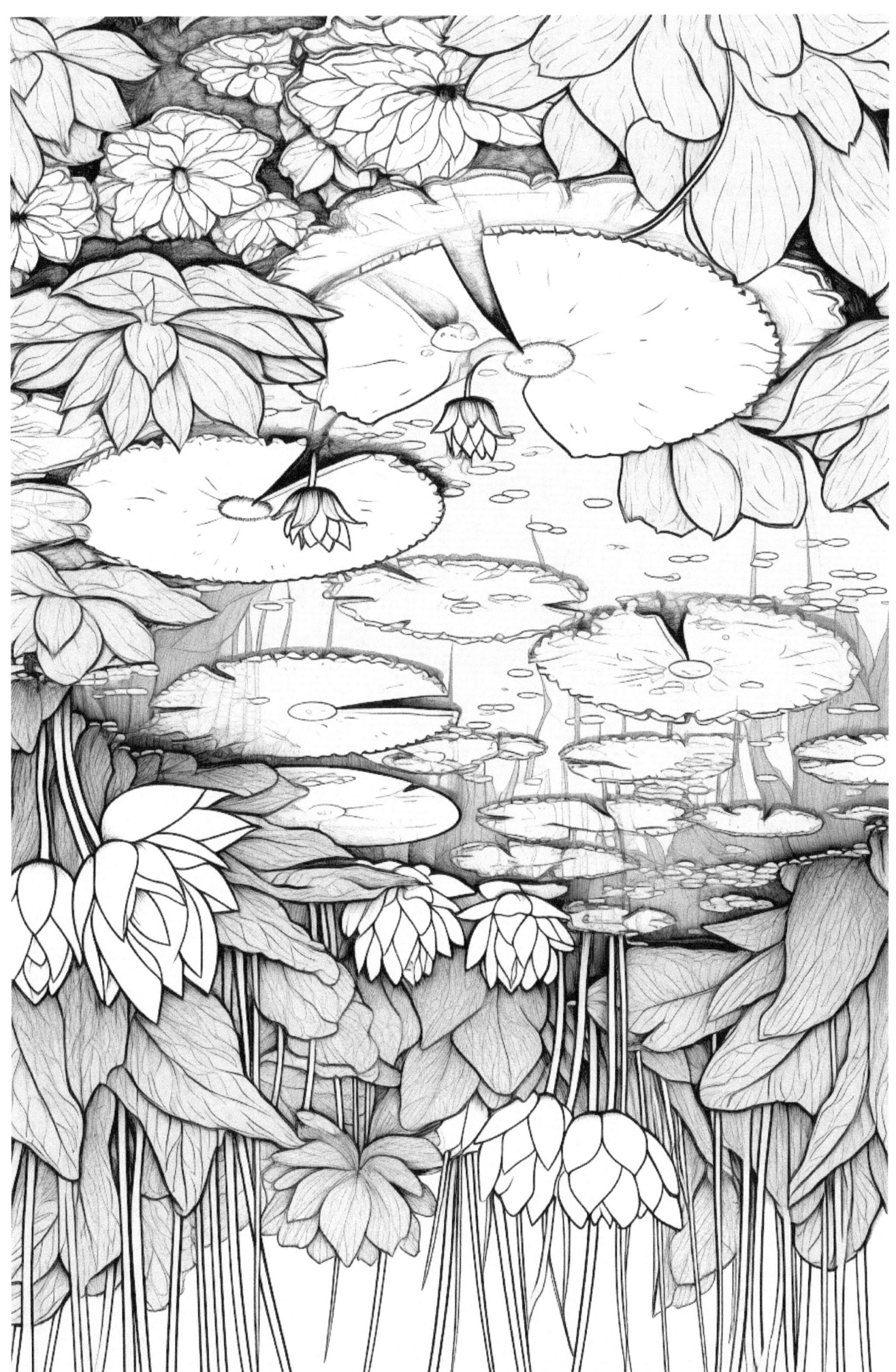

Fairies left this blank for you

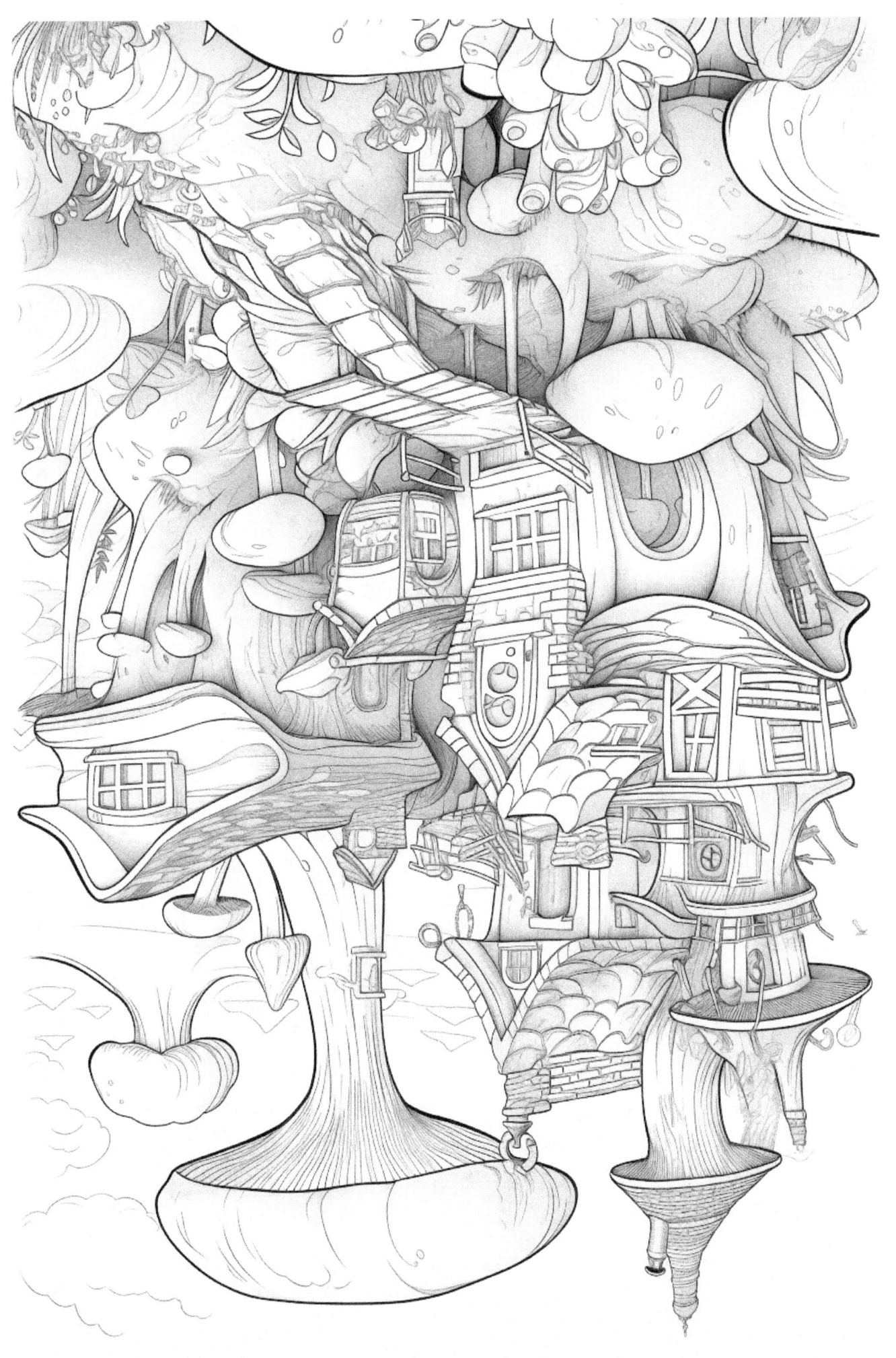

Fairies left this blank for you

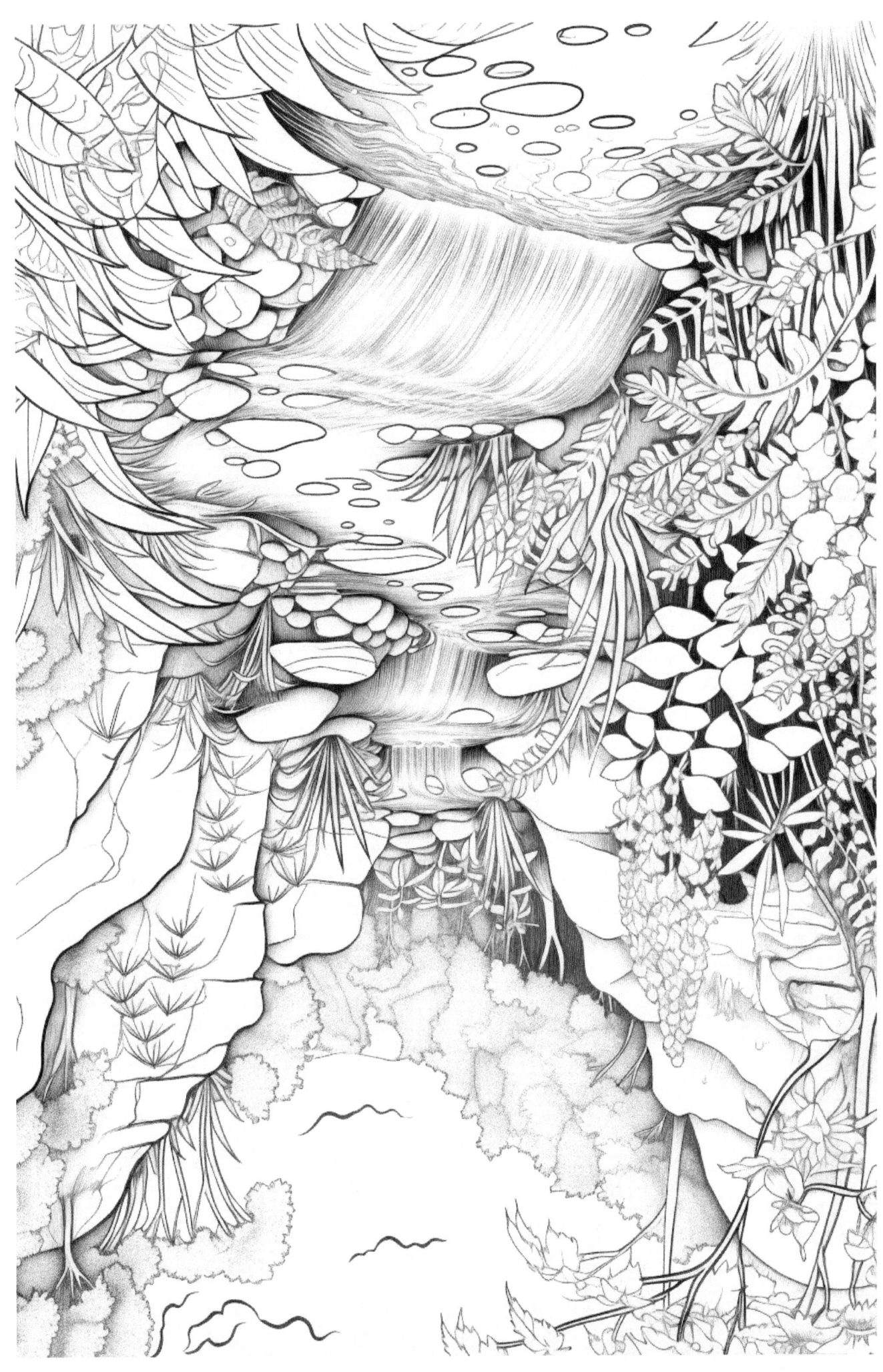

Fairies left this blank for you

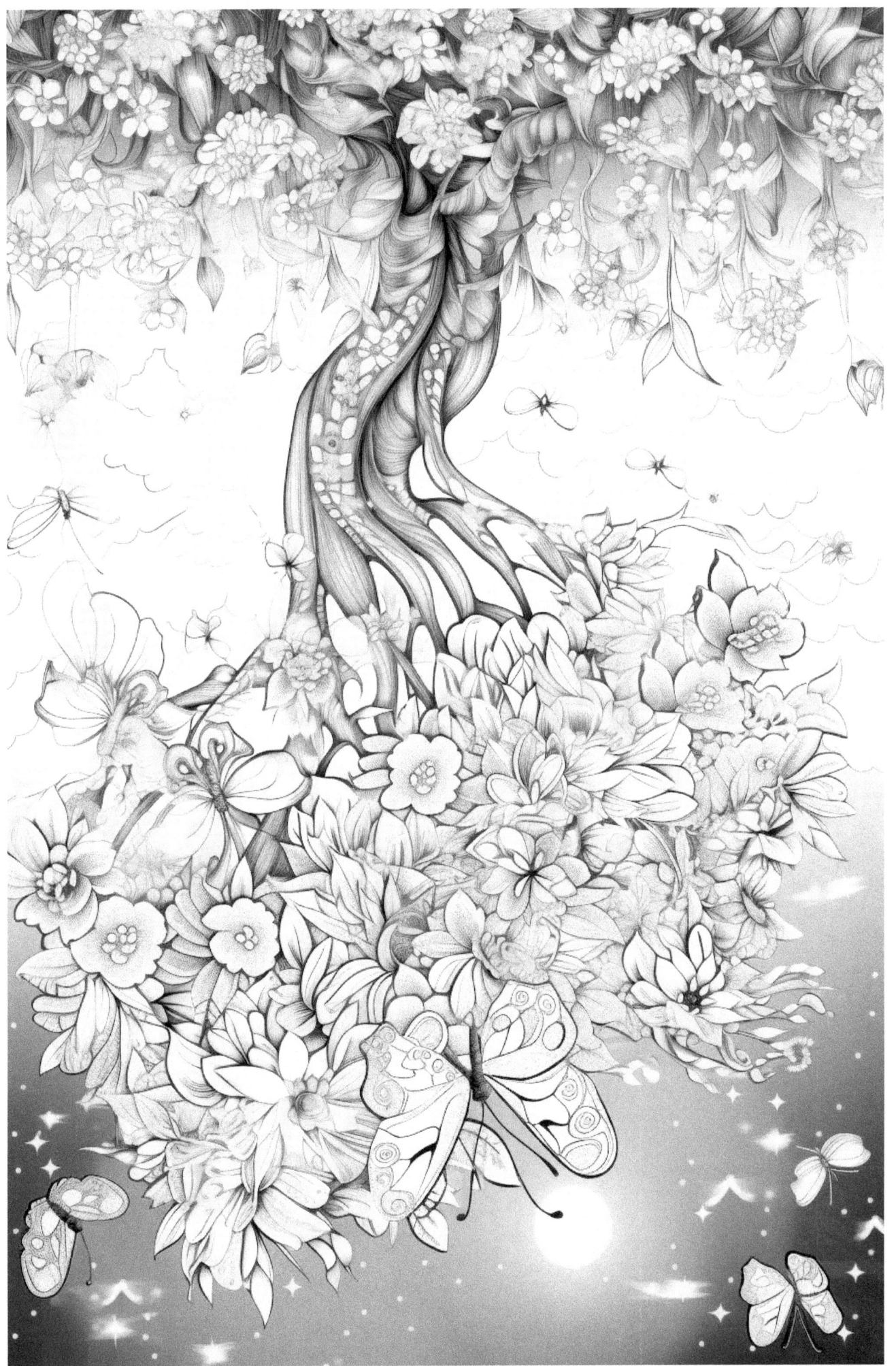

Fairies left this blank for you

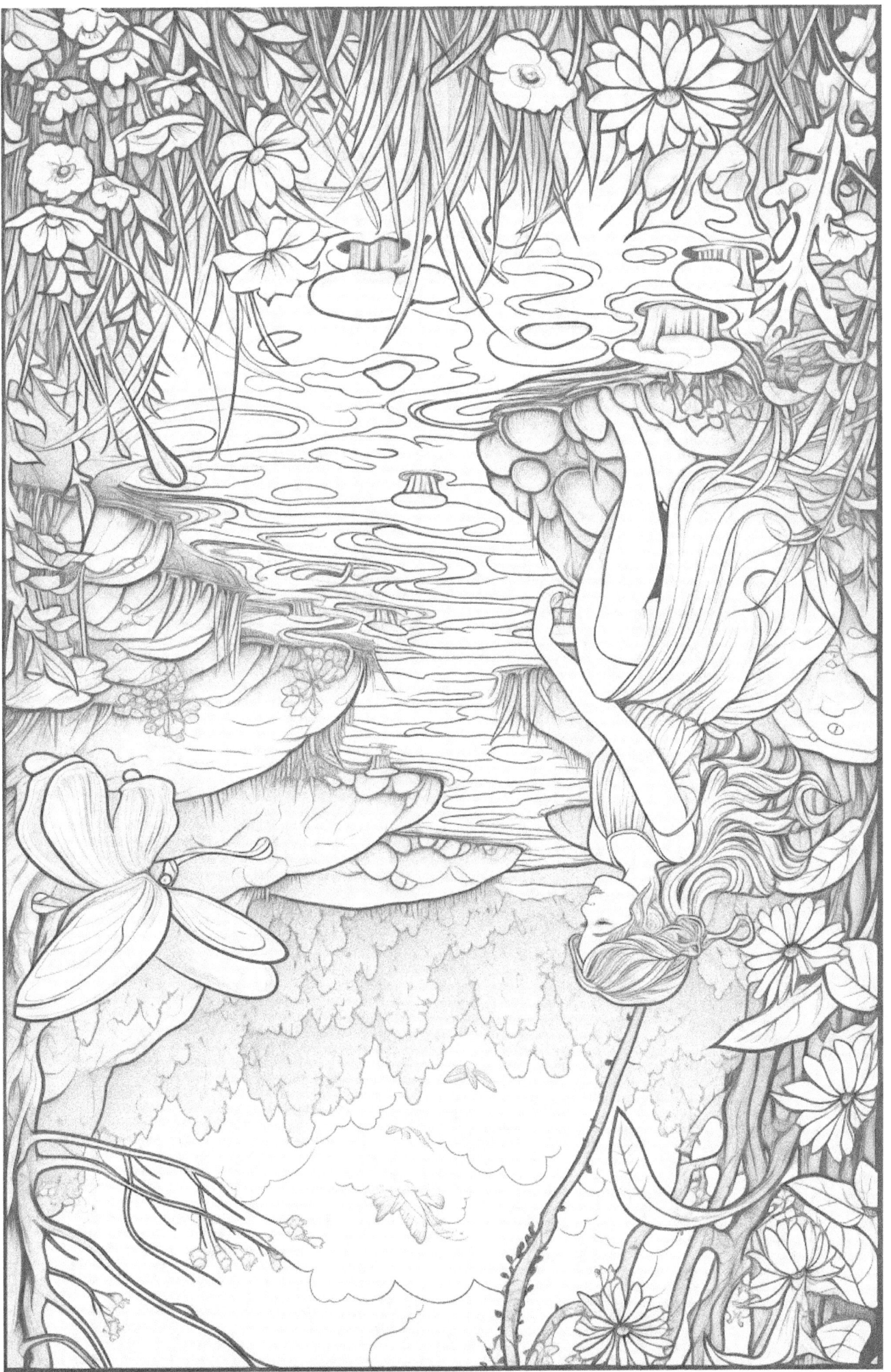

Fairies left this blank for you

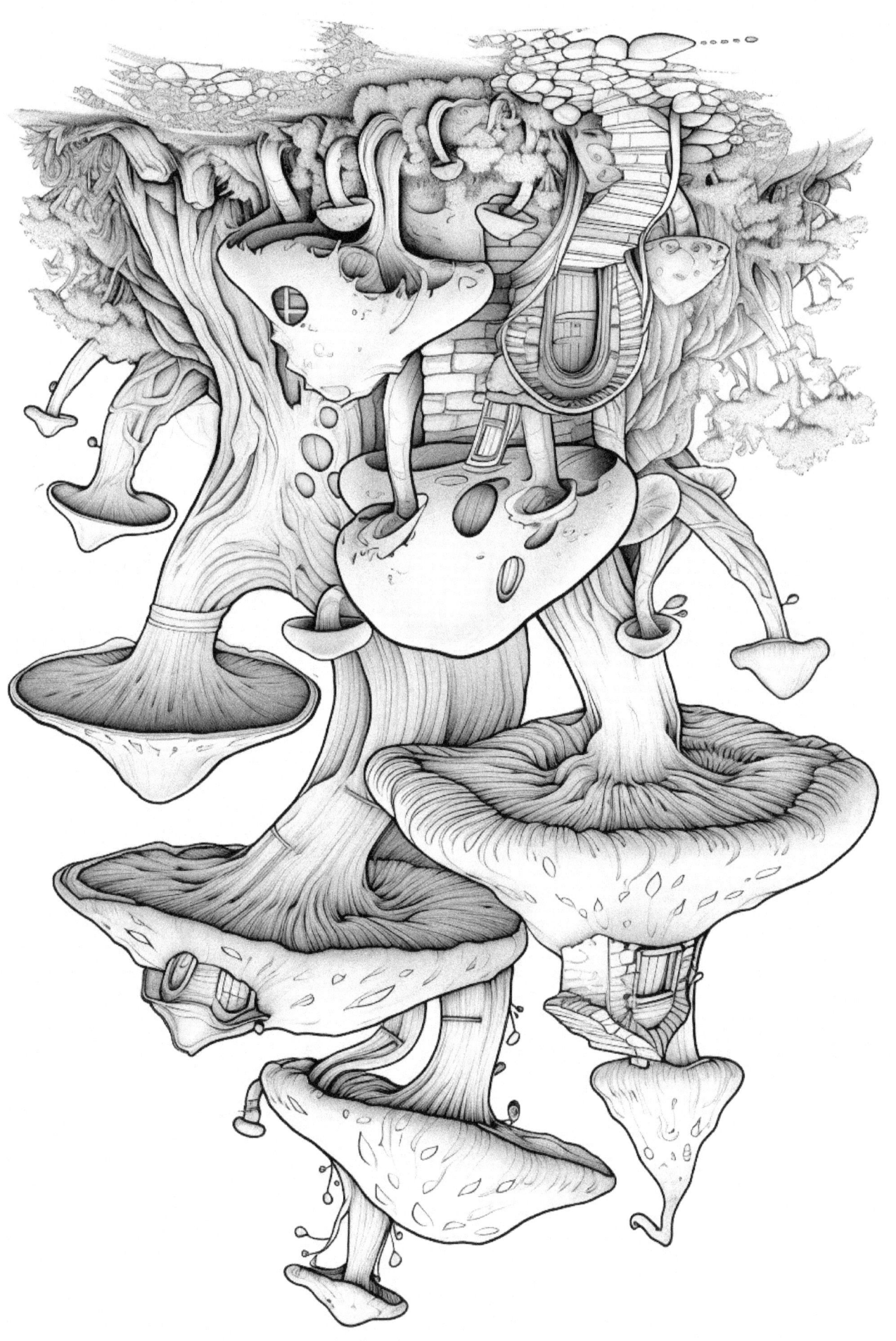

Fairies left this blank for you

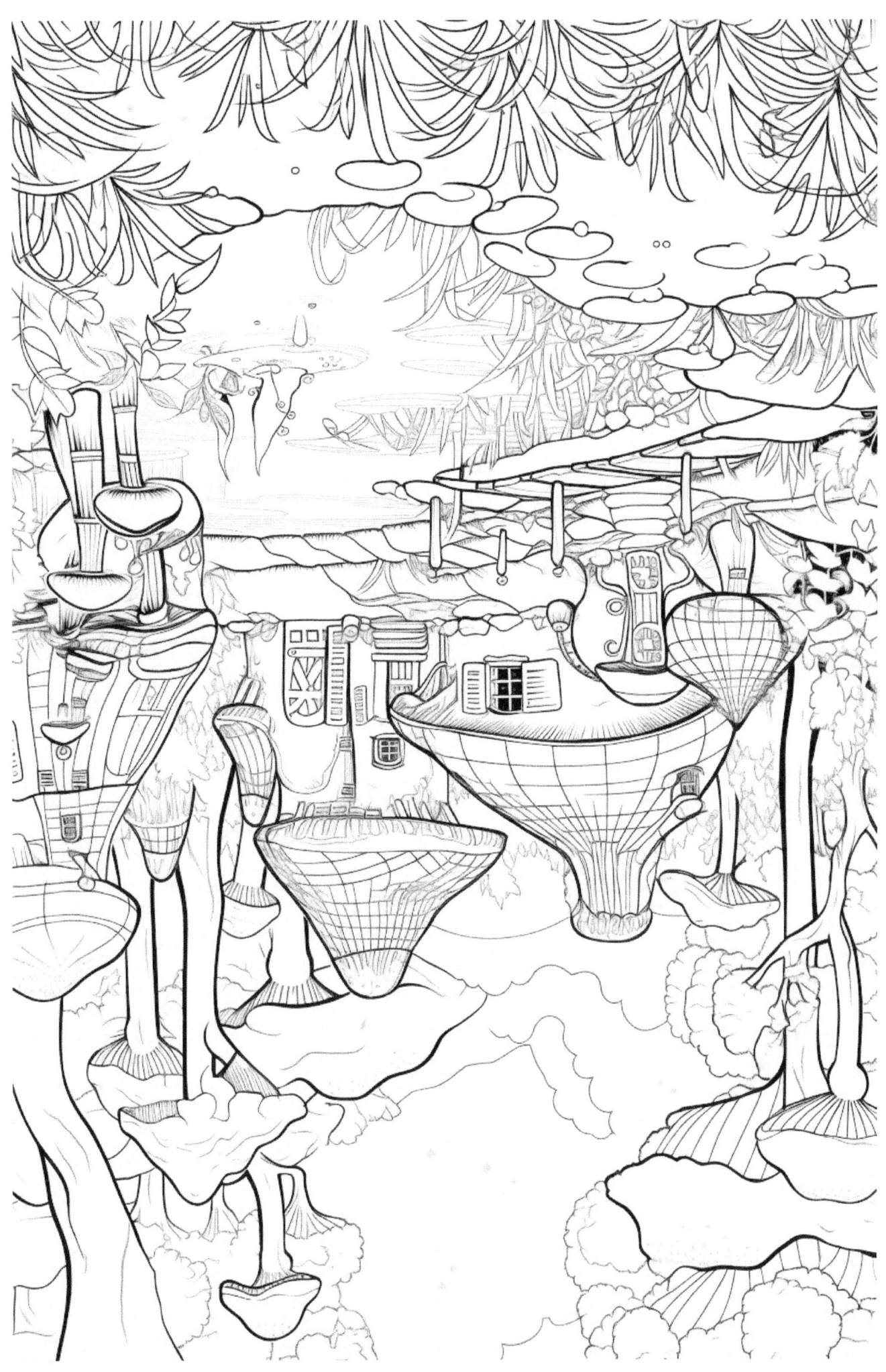

Fairies left this blank for you

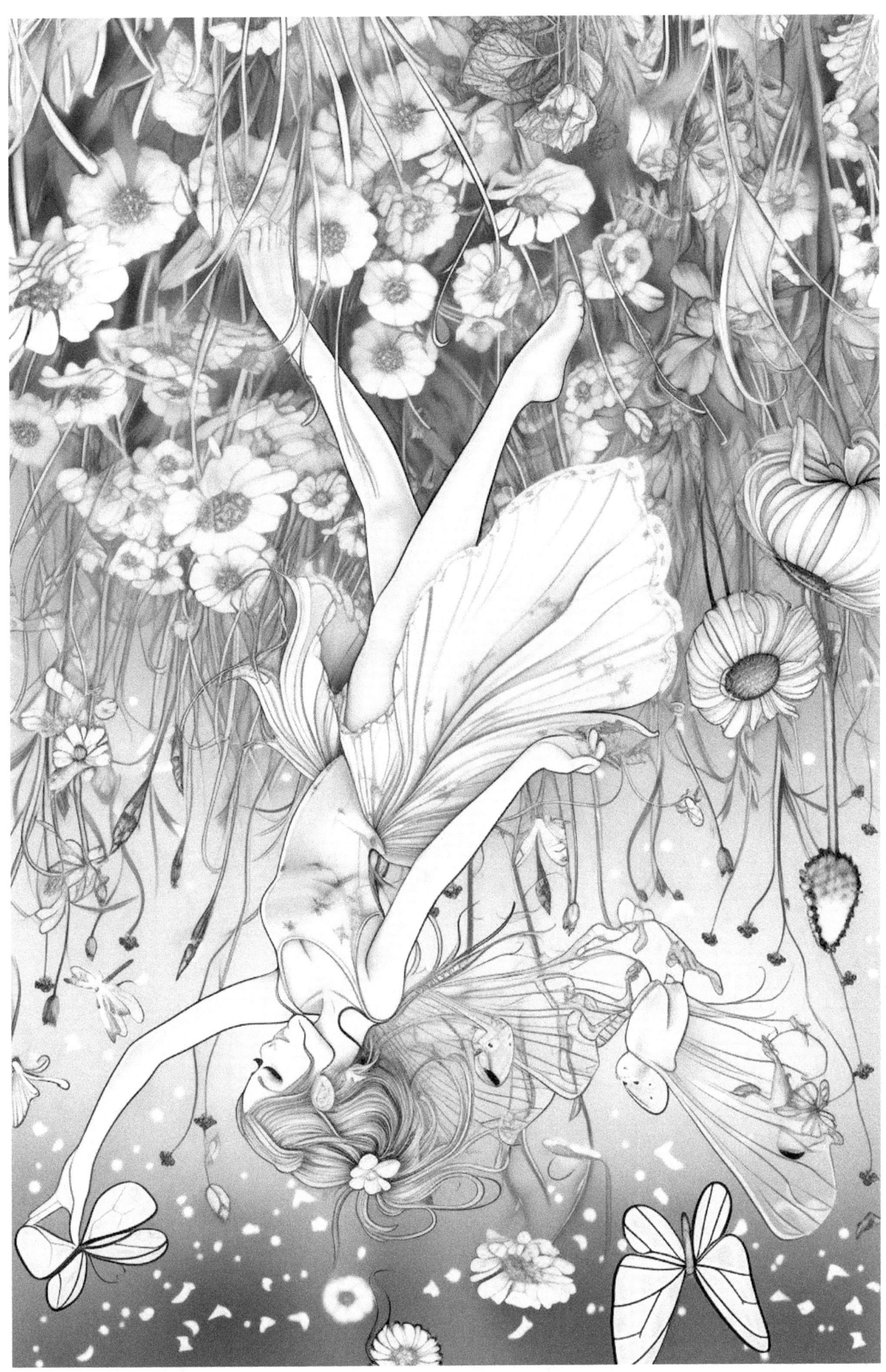

Fairies left this blank for you

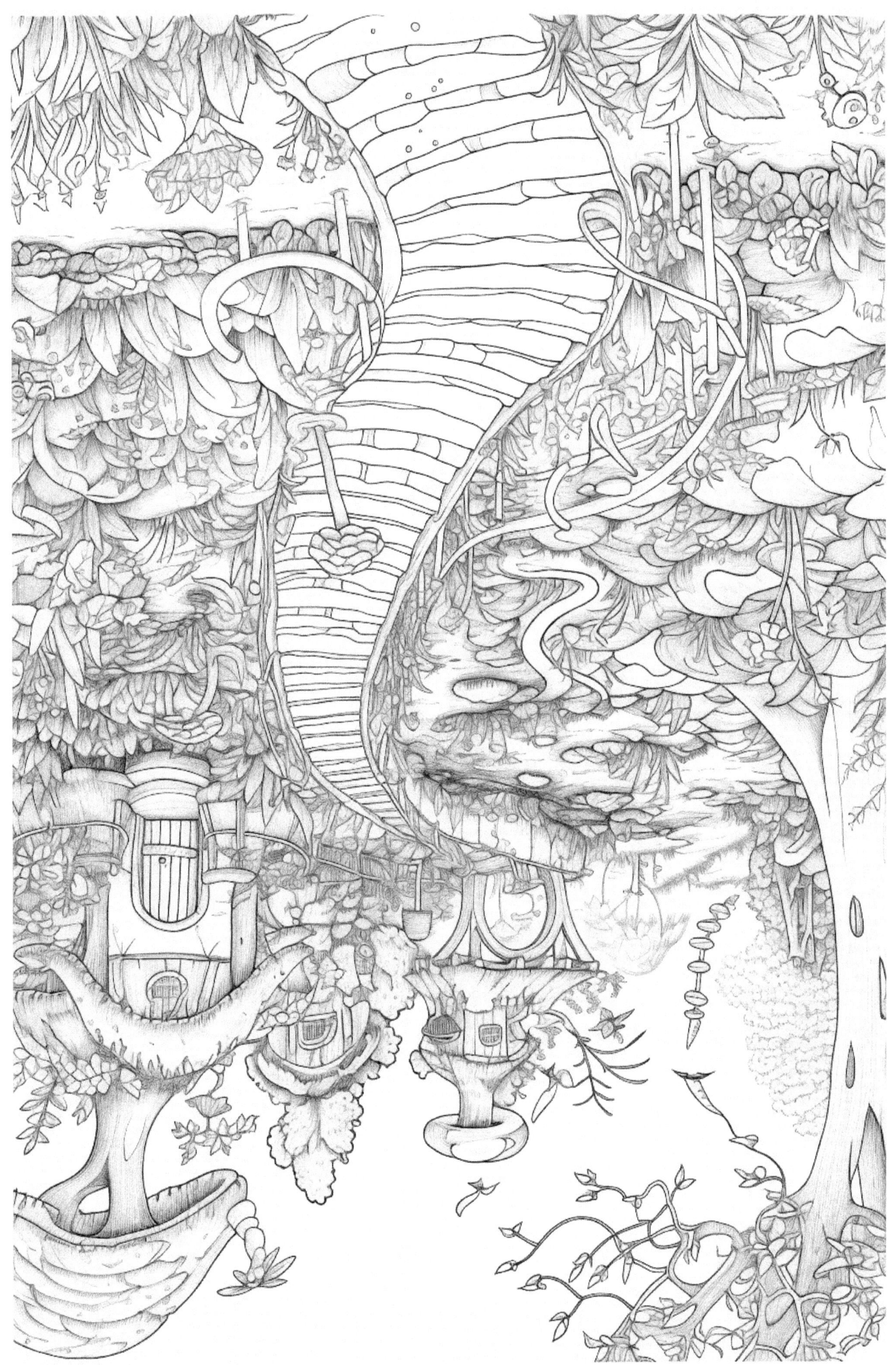

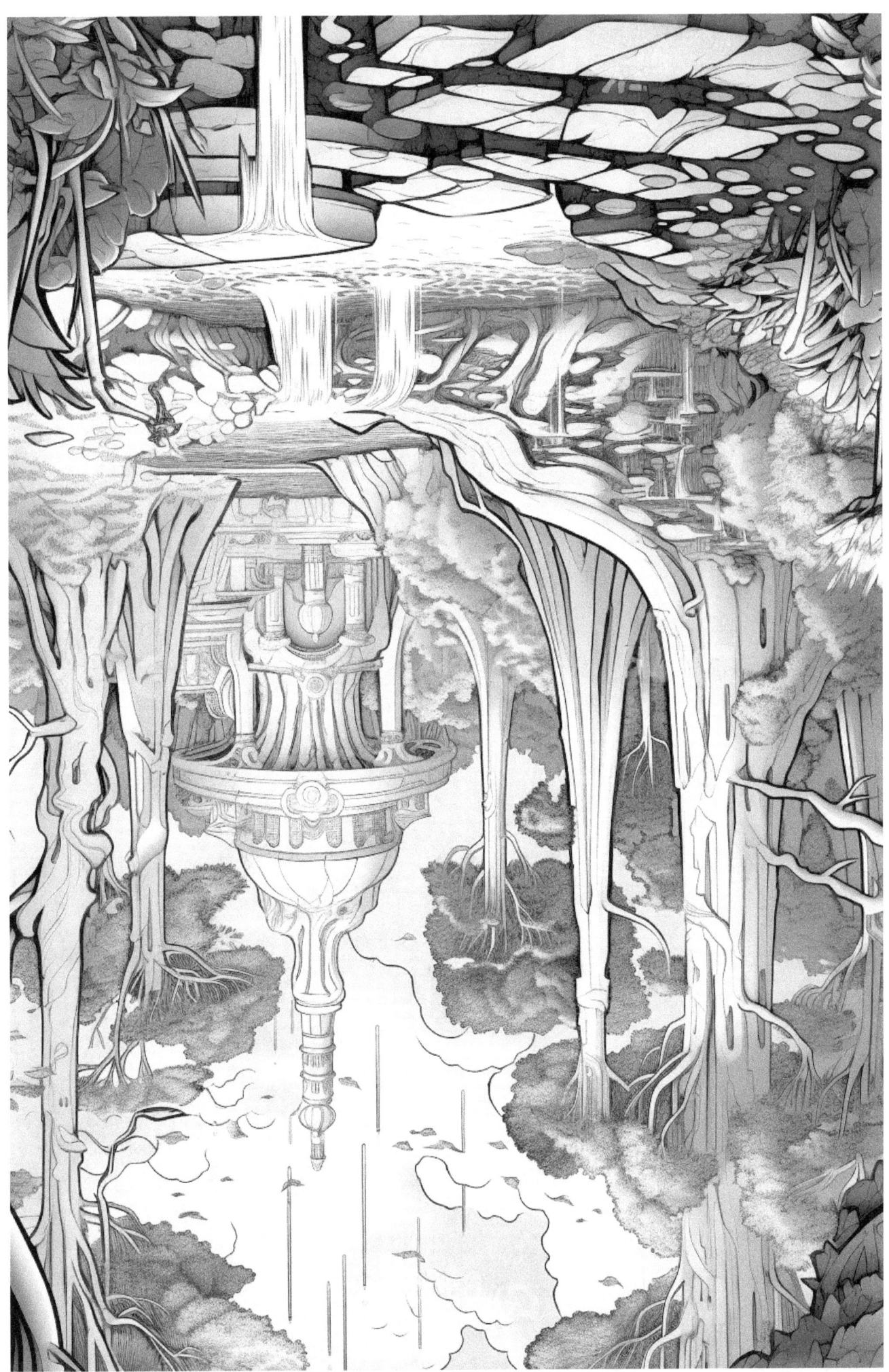

Fairies left this blank for you

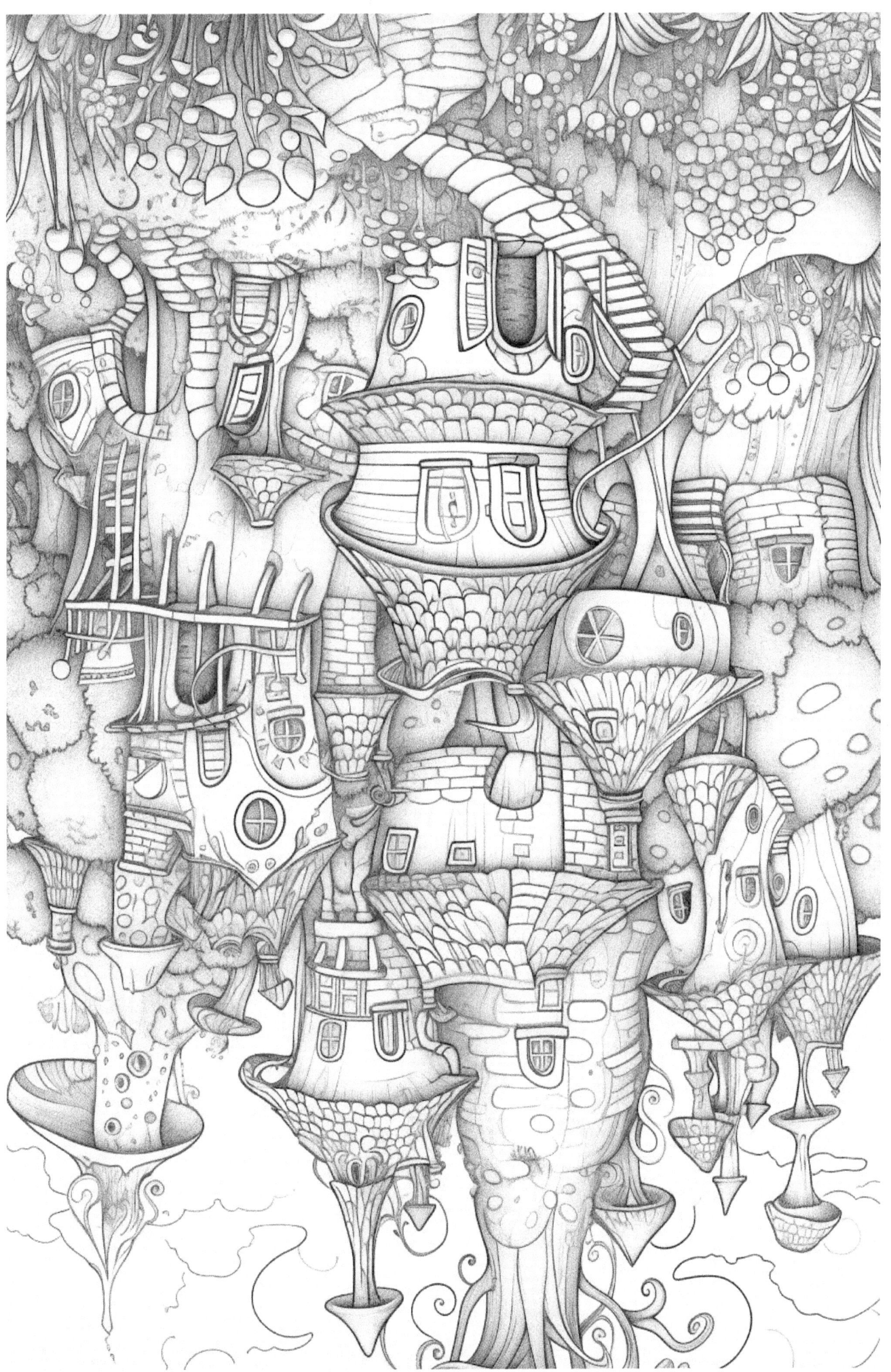

Fairies left this blank for you

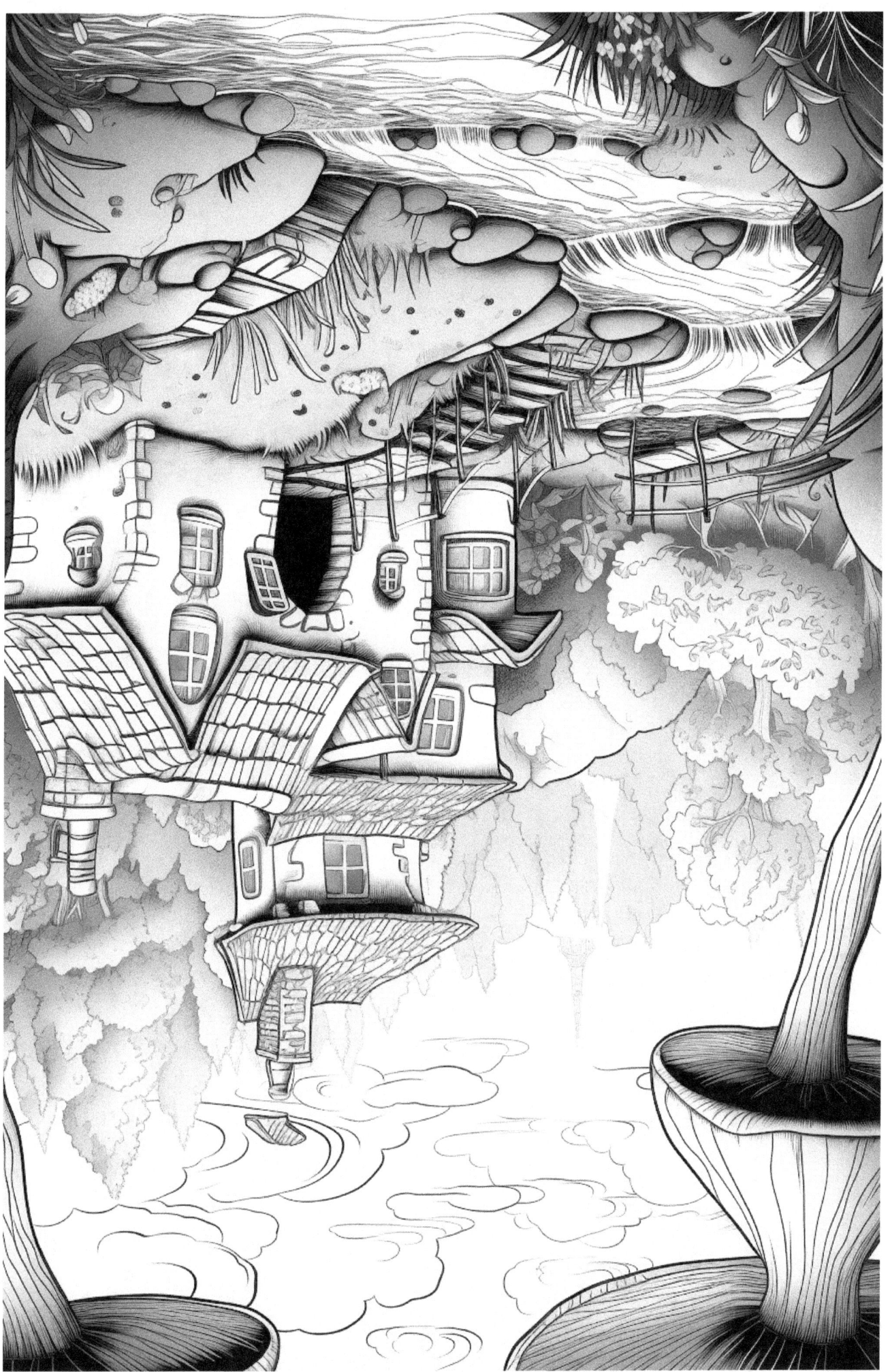

Fairies left this blank for you

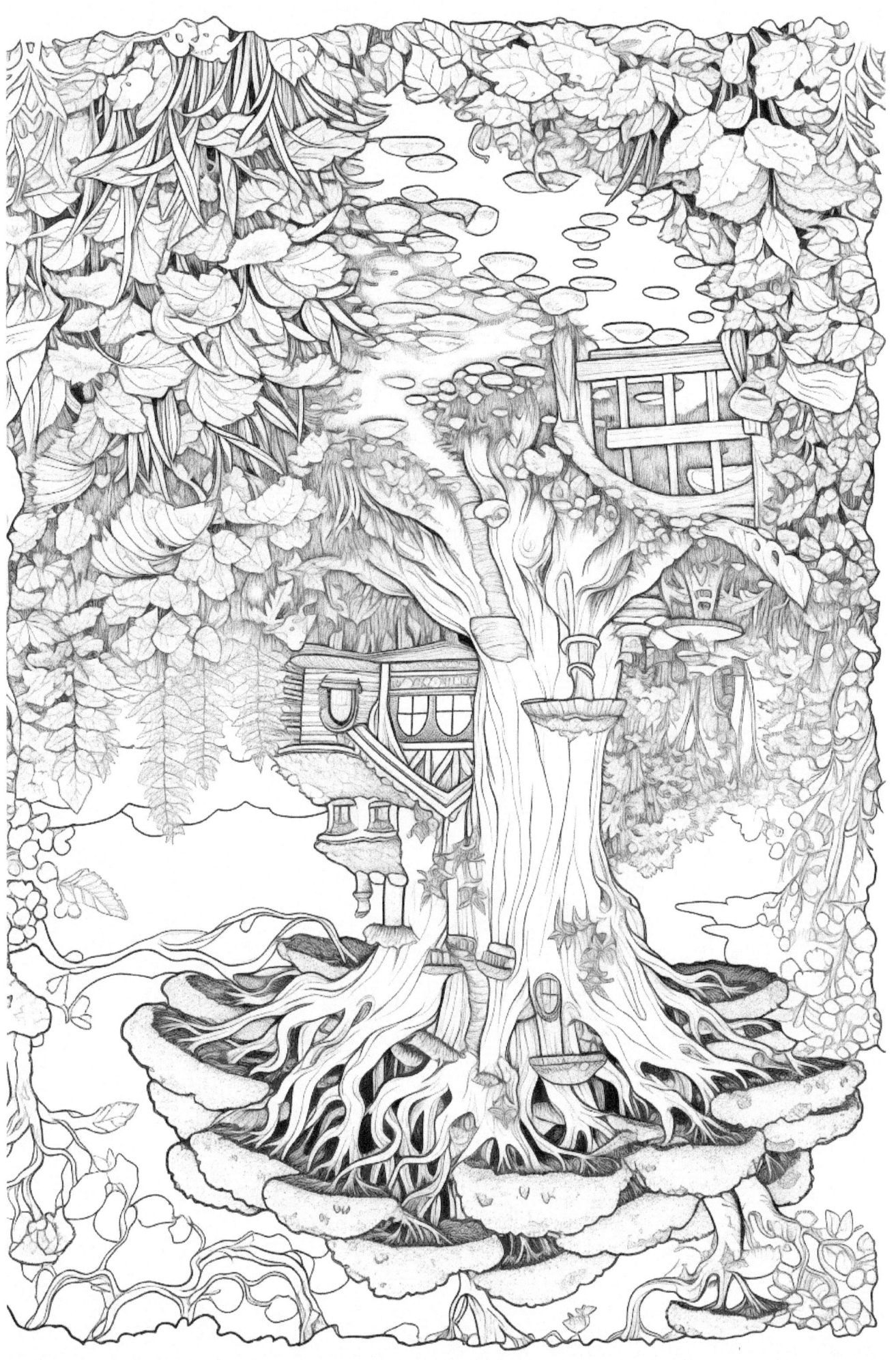

Fairies left this blank for you

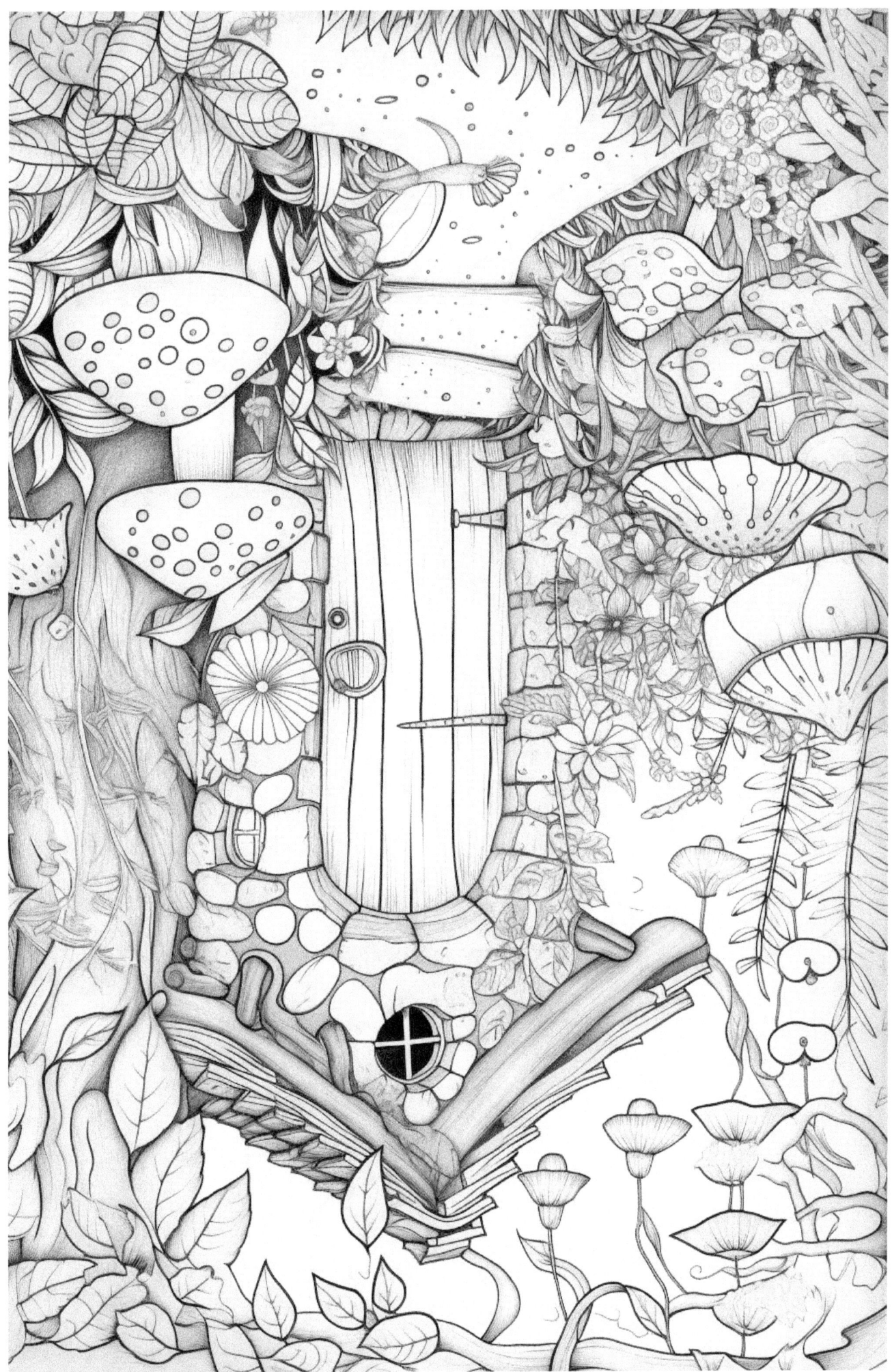

Fairies left this blank for you

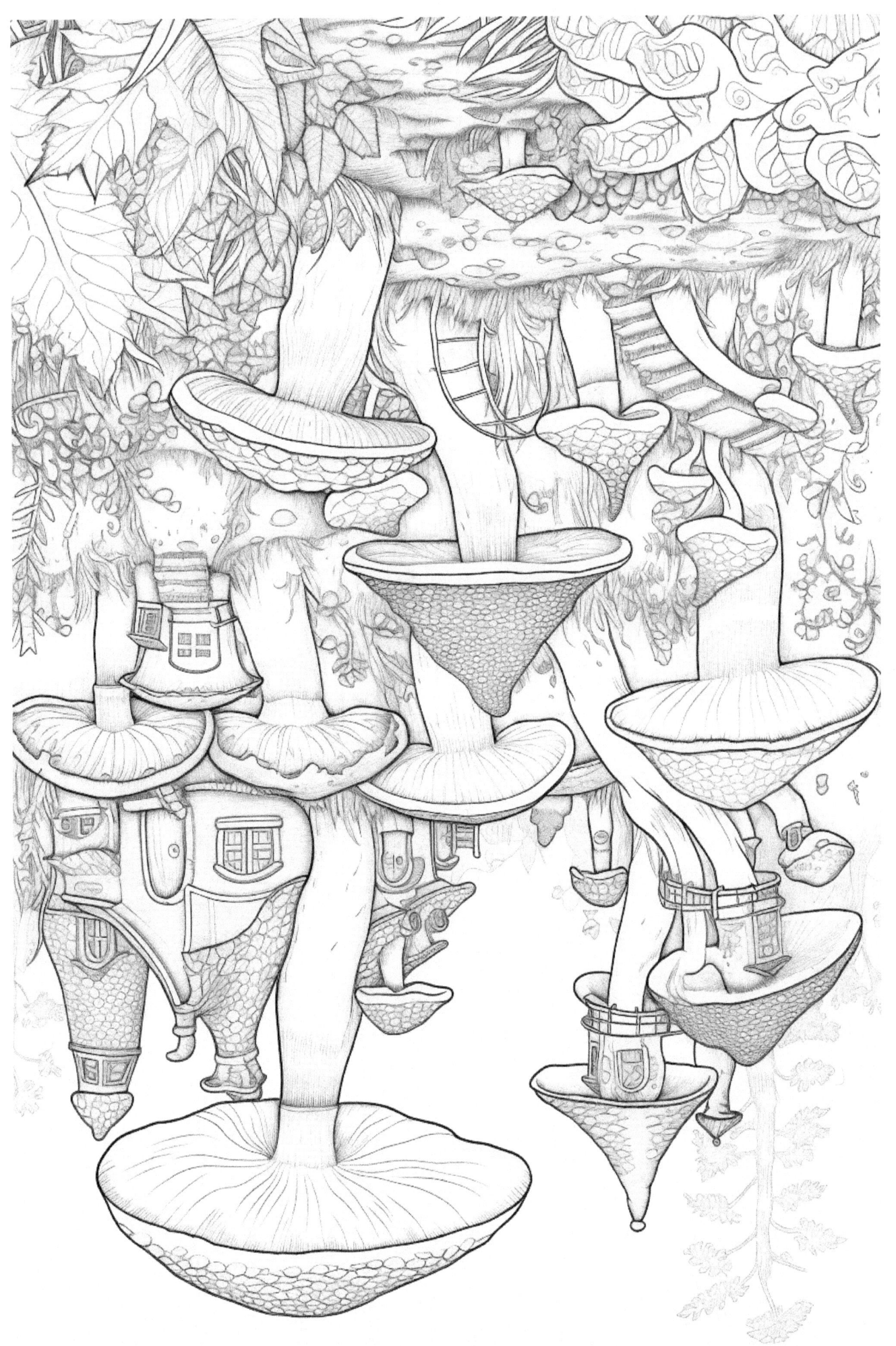

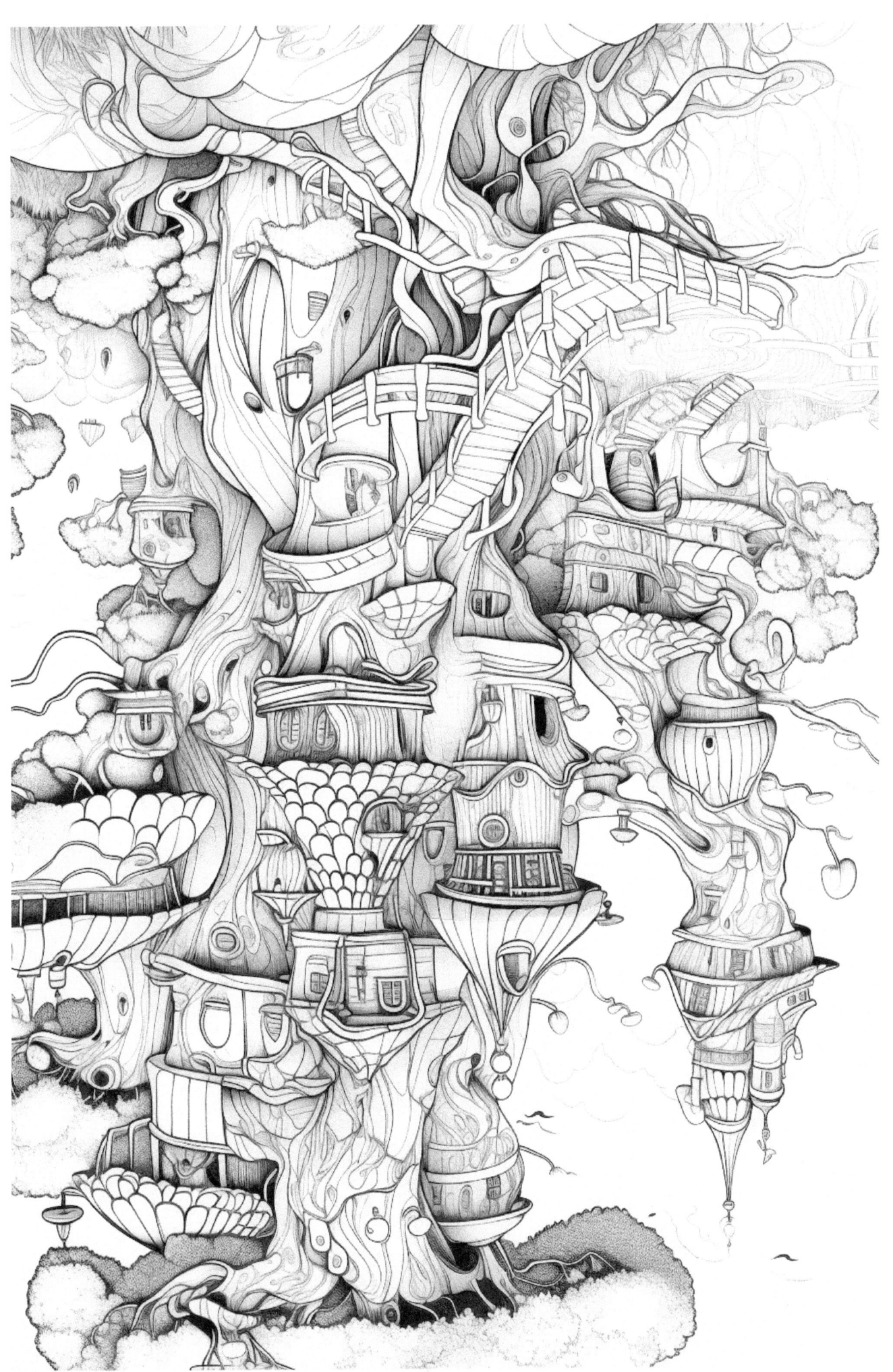

Fairies left this blank for you

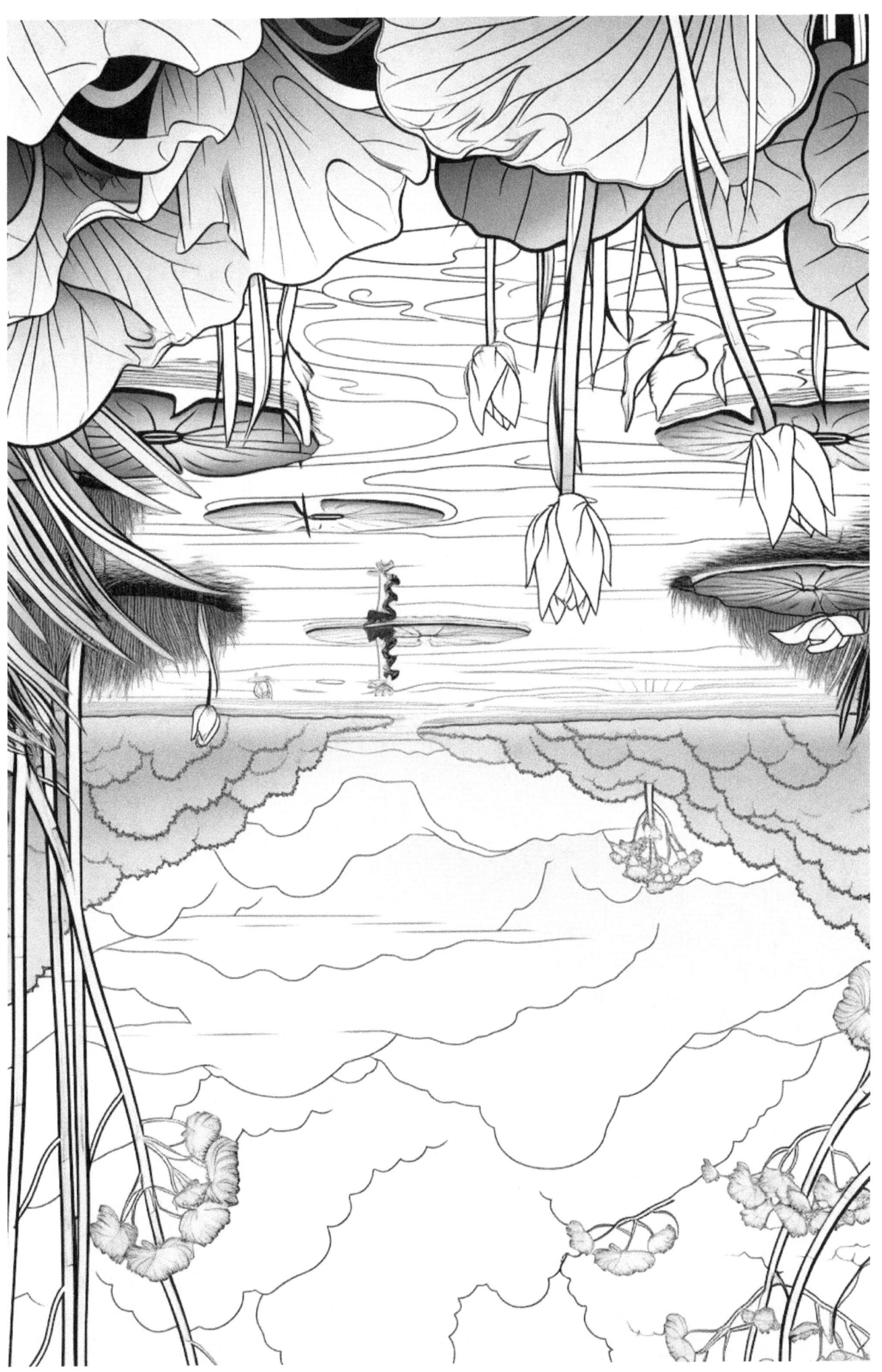

Fairies left this blank for you

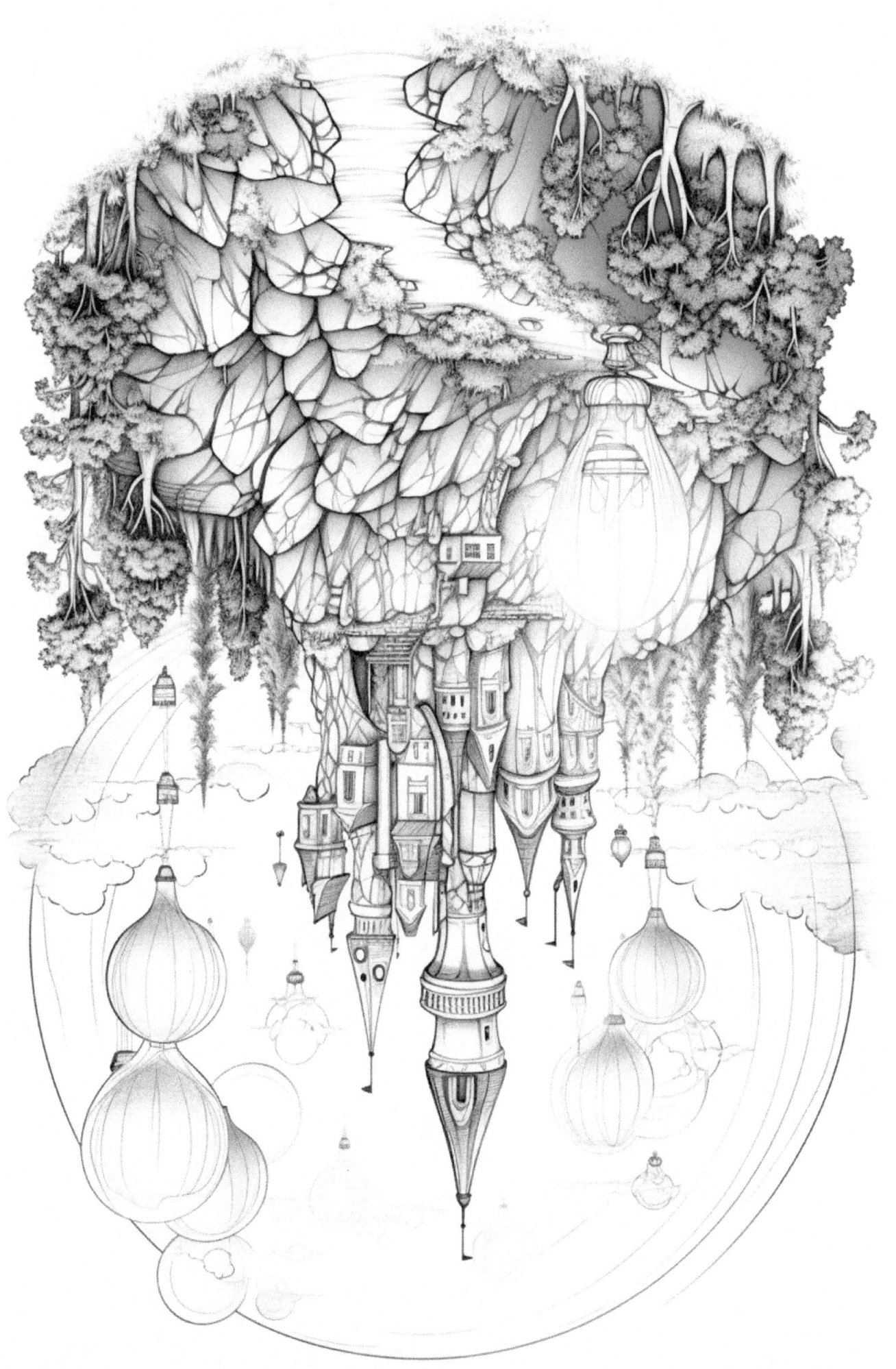

Fairies left this blank for you

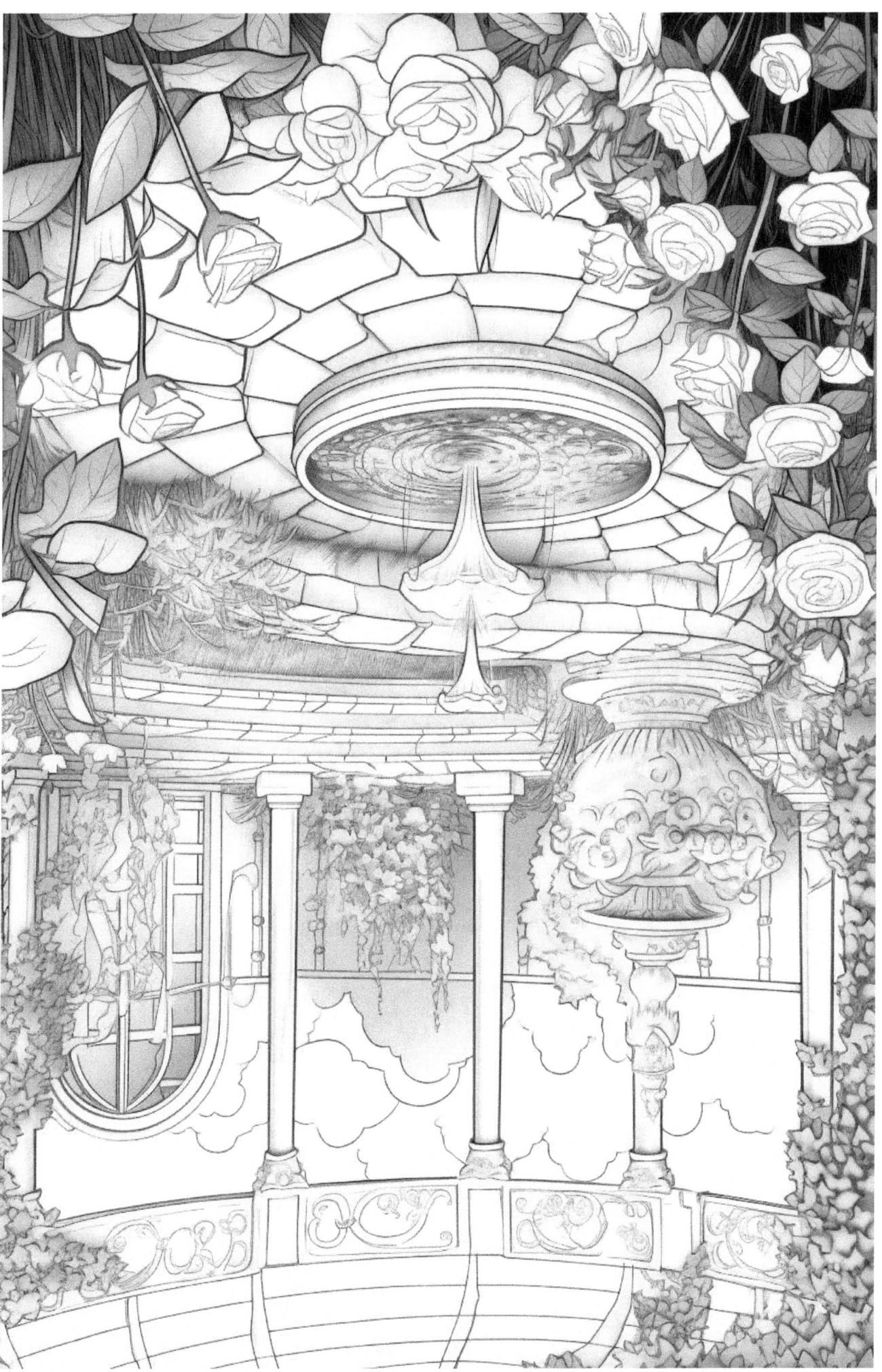

Fairies left this blank for you

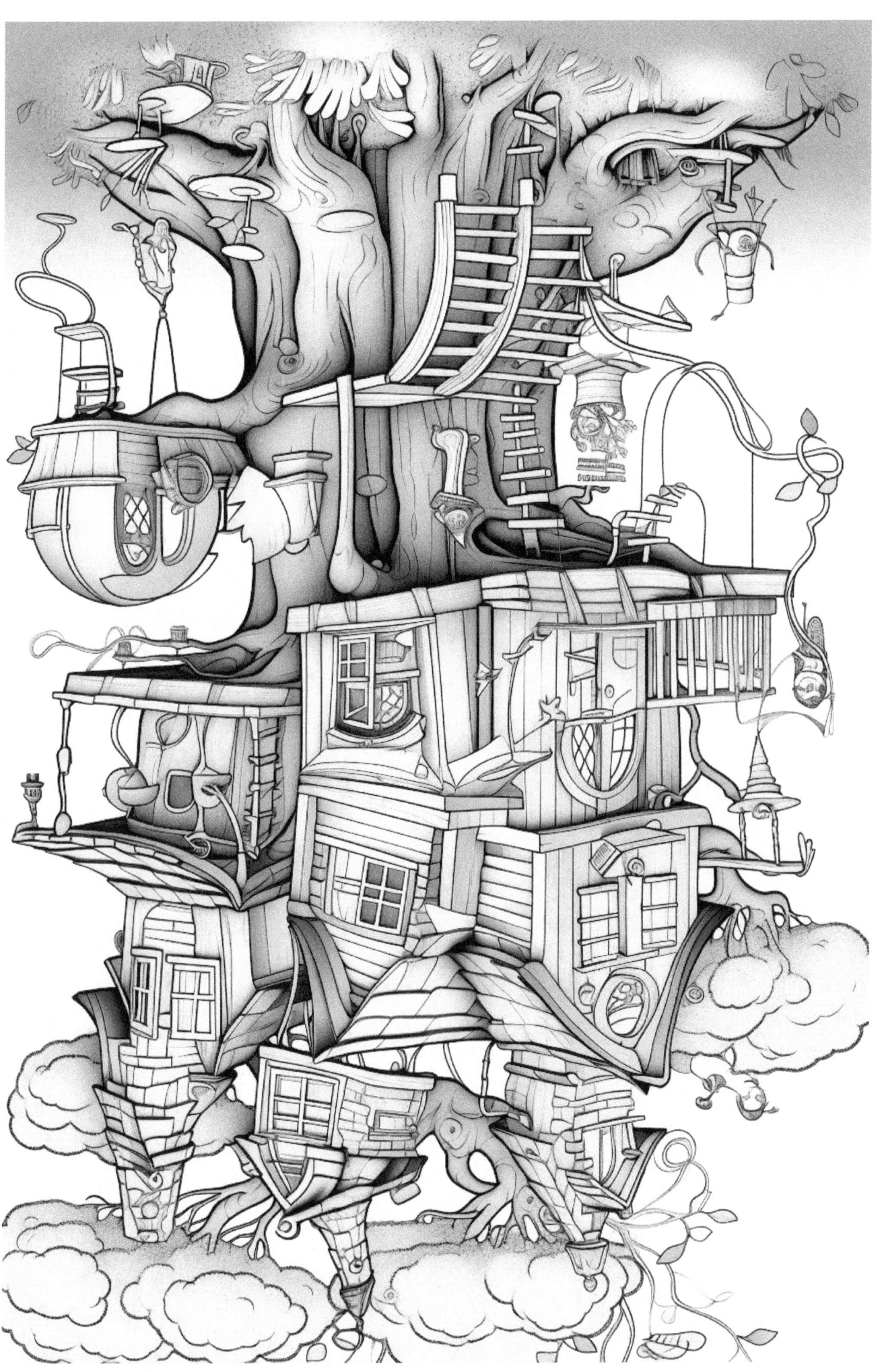

Fairies left this blank for you

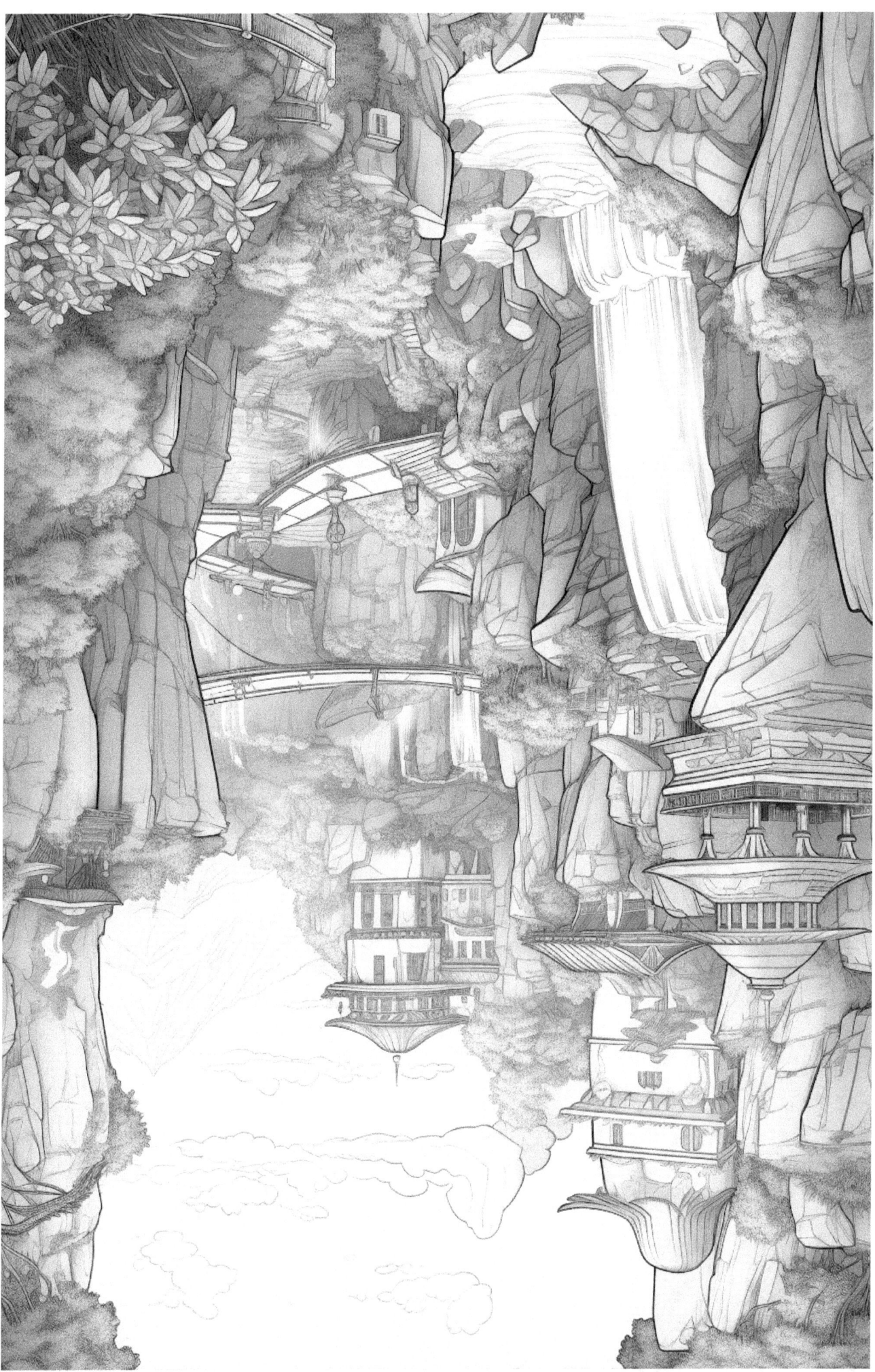

Fairies left this blank for you

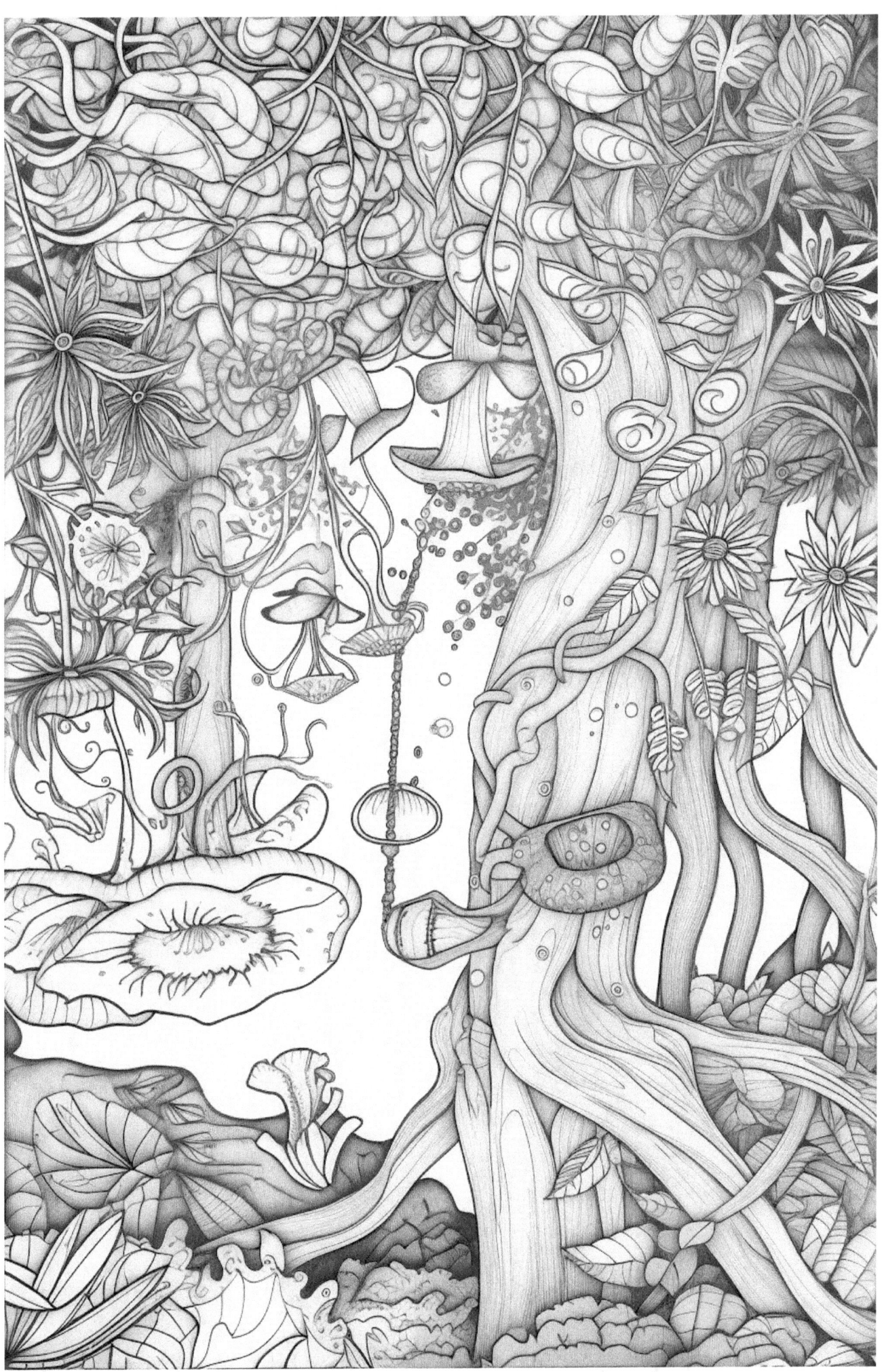

Fairies left this blank for you

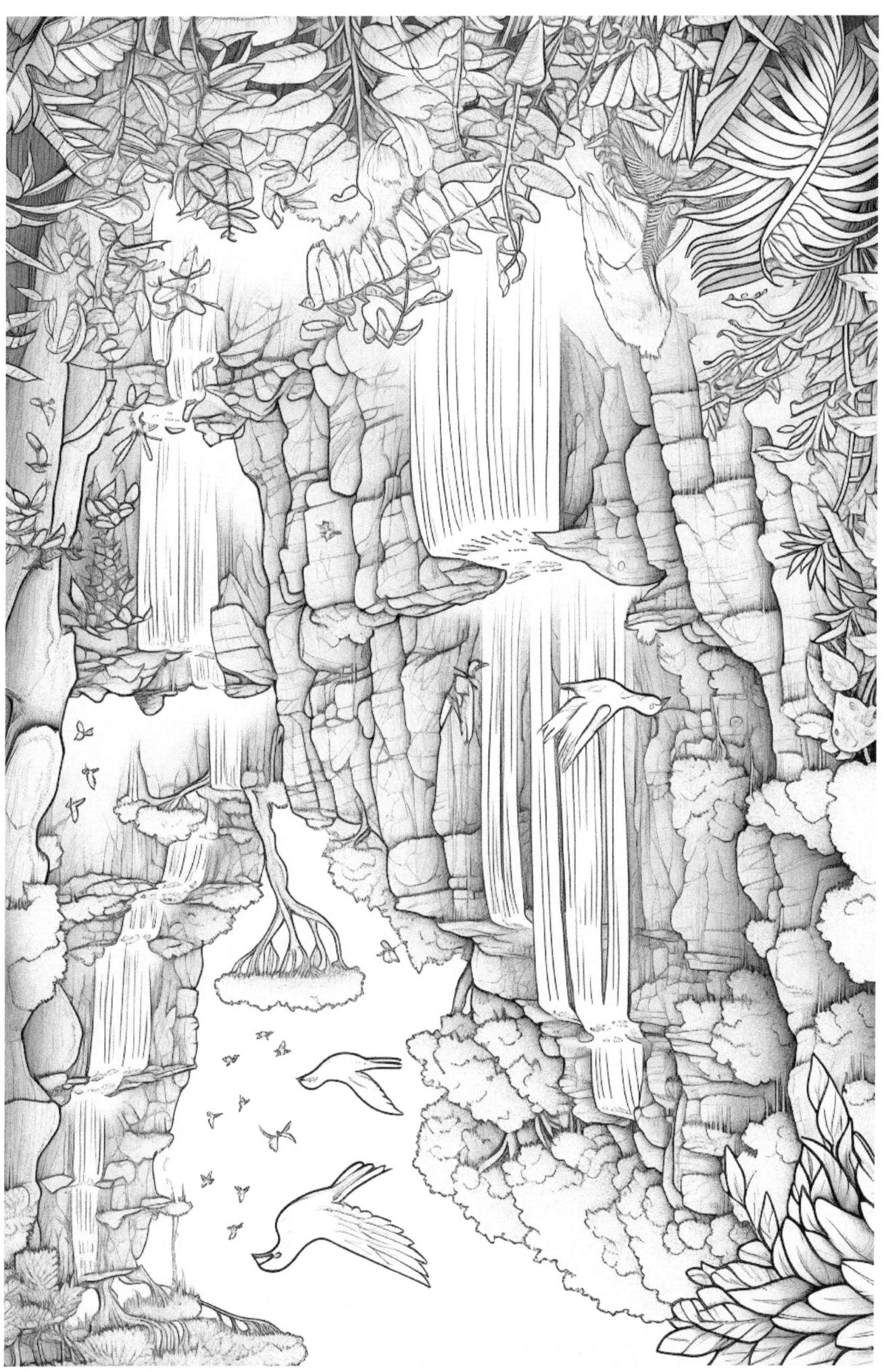

Fairies left this blank for you

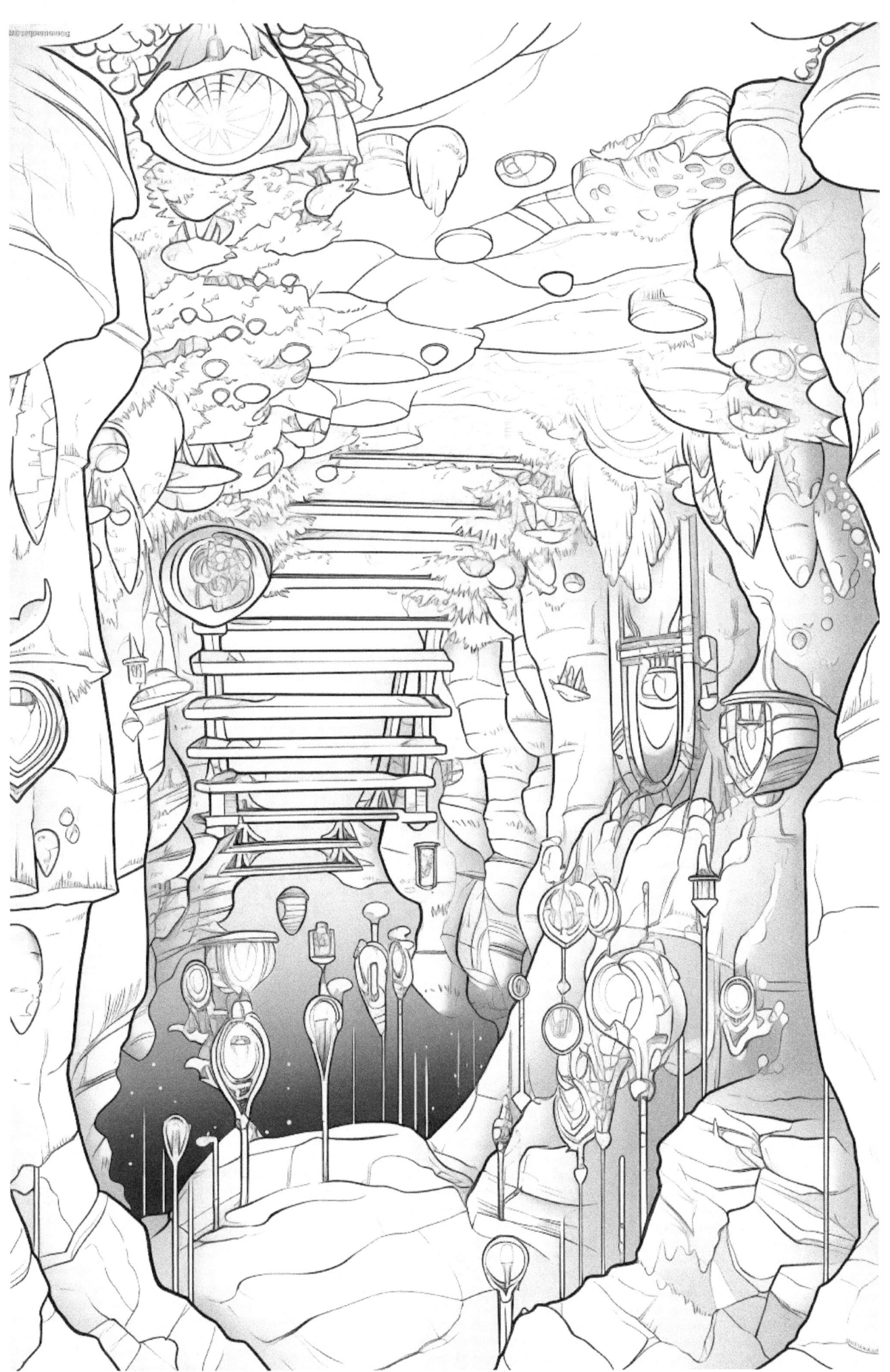

Fairies left this blank for you

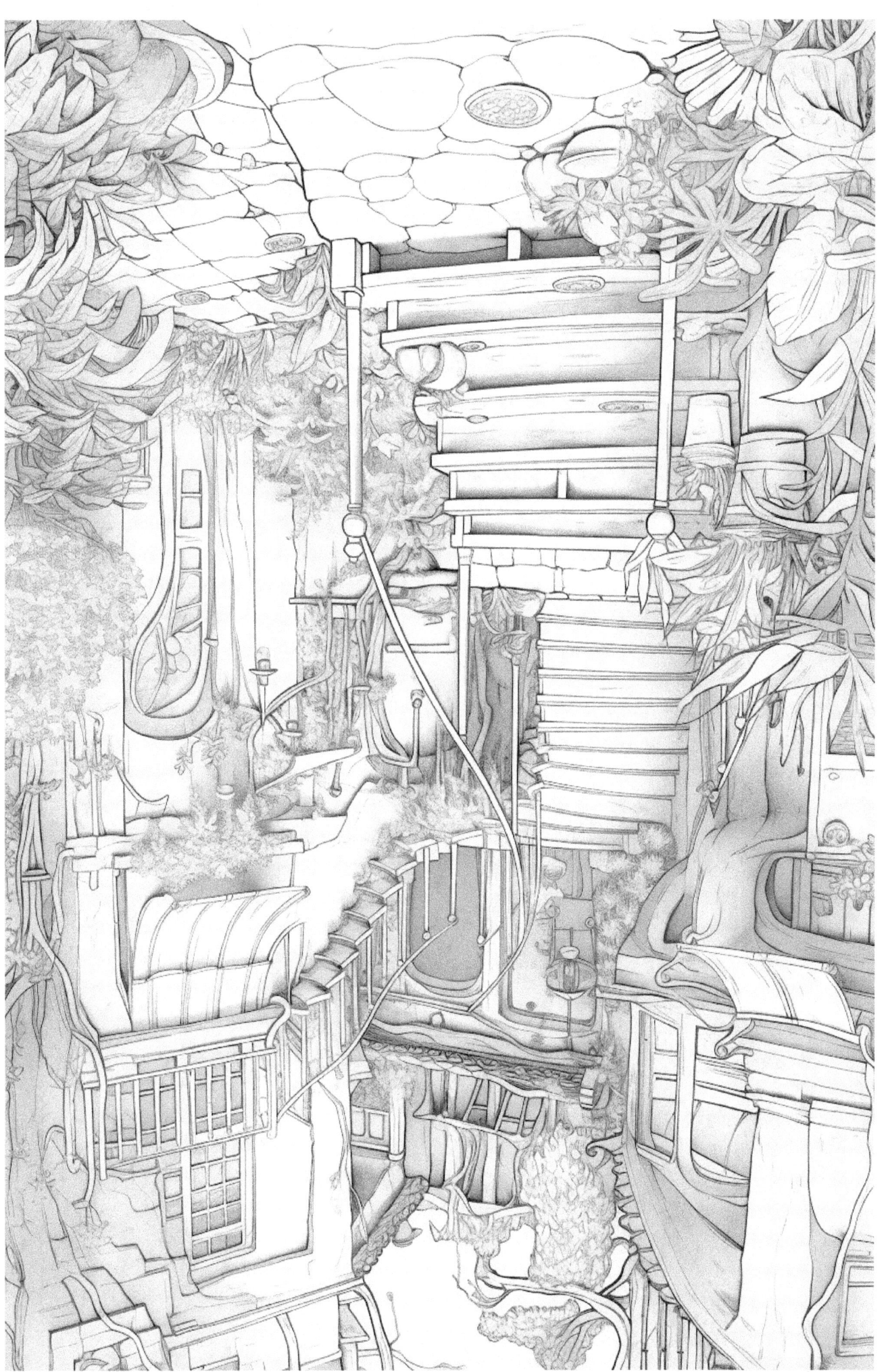

Fairies left this blank for you

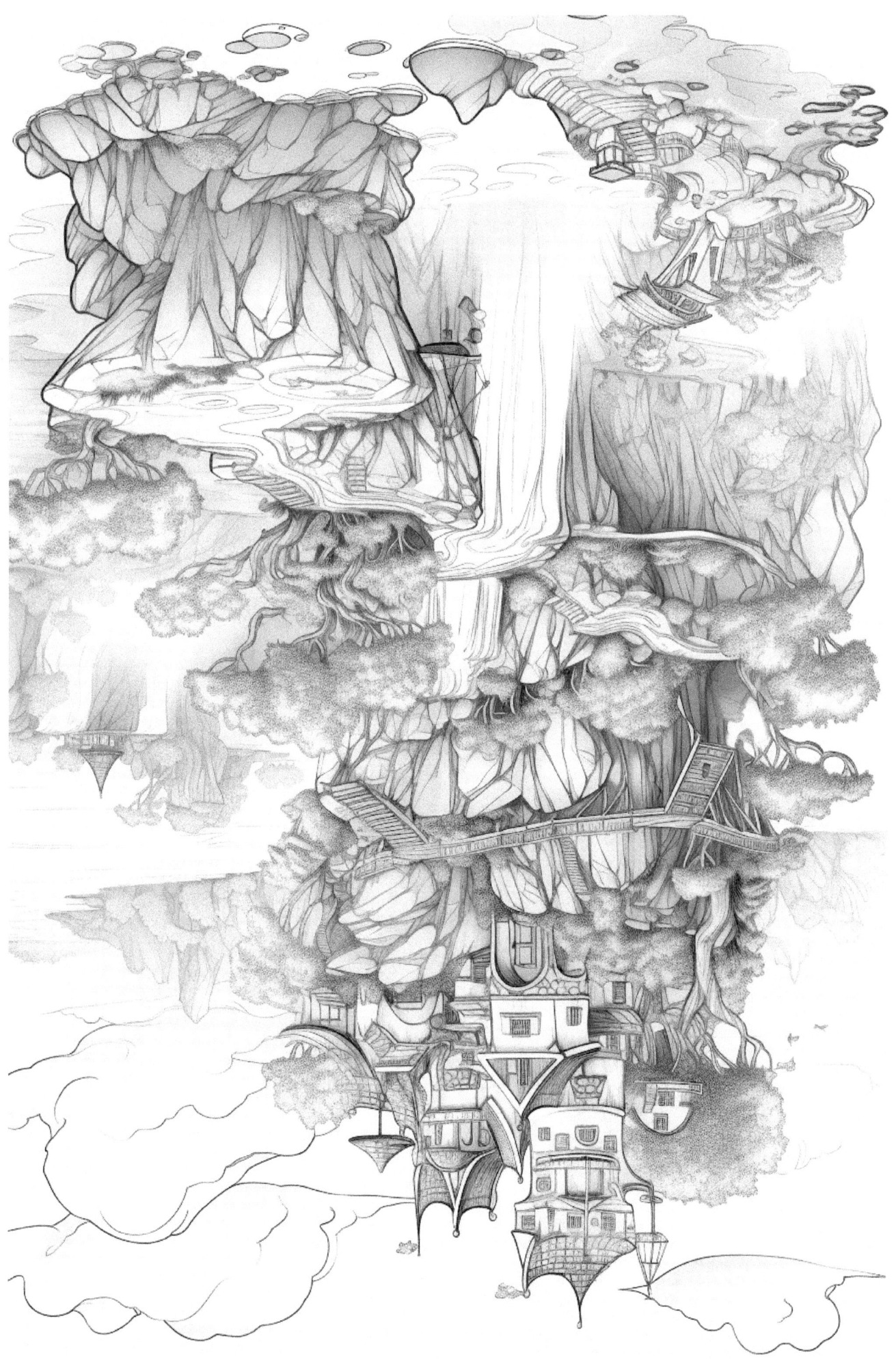

Fairies left this blank for you

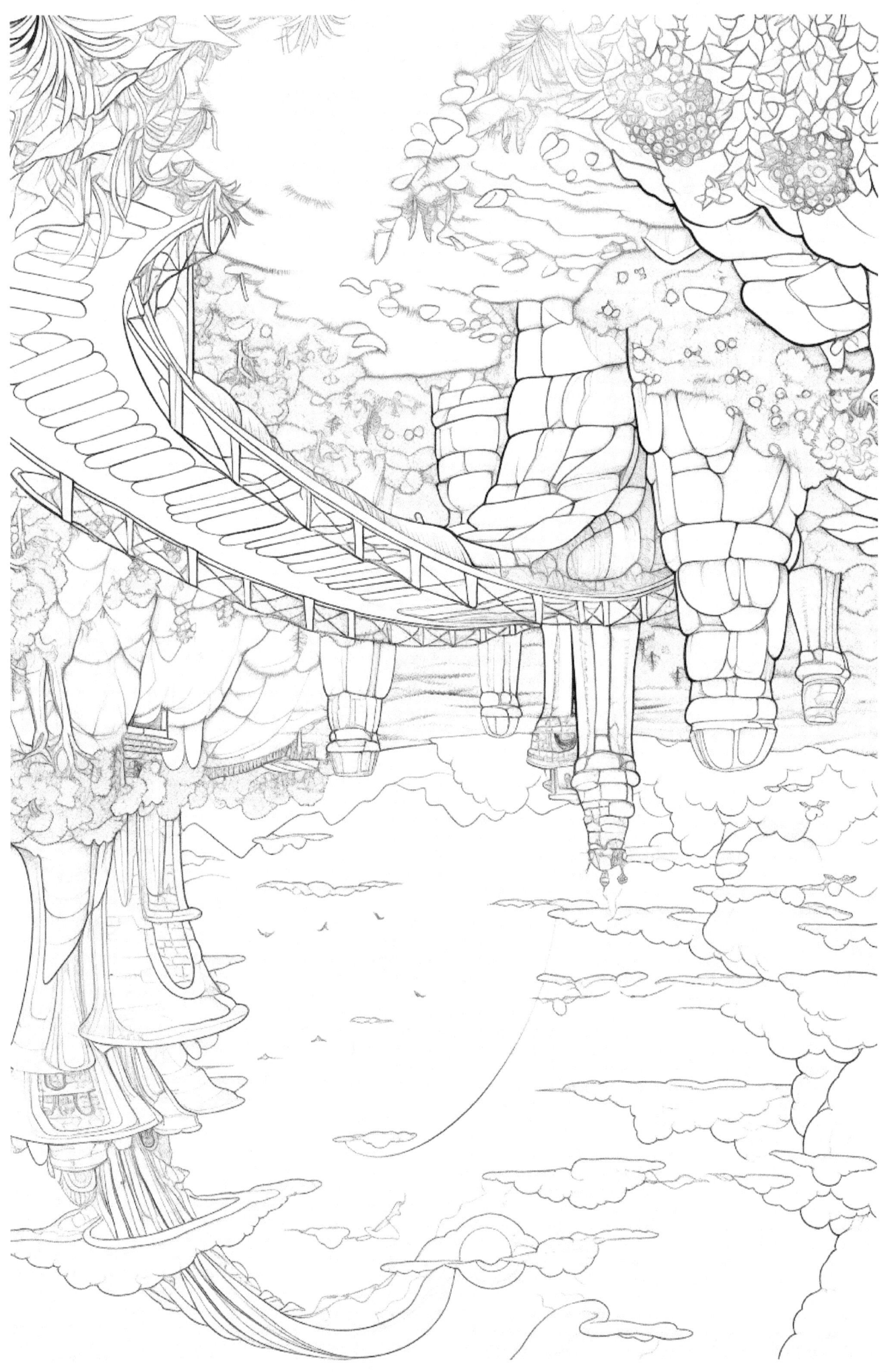

Fairies left this blank for you

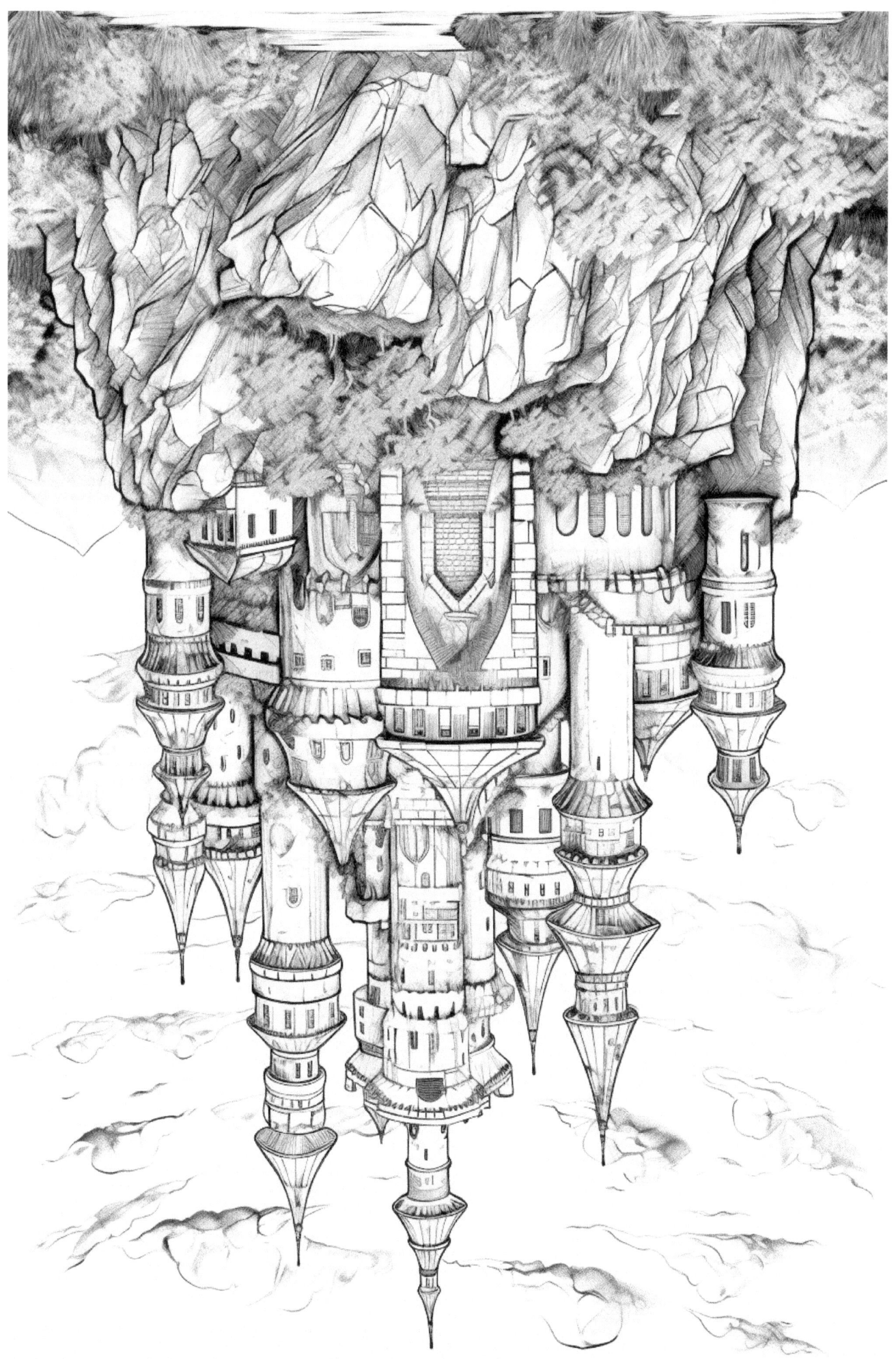

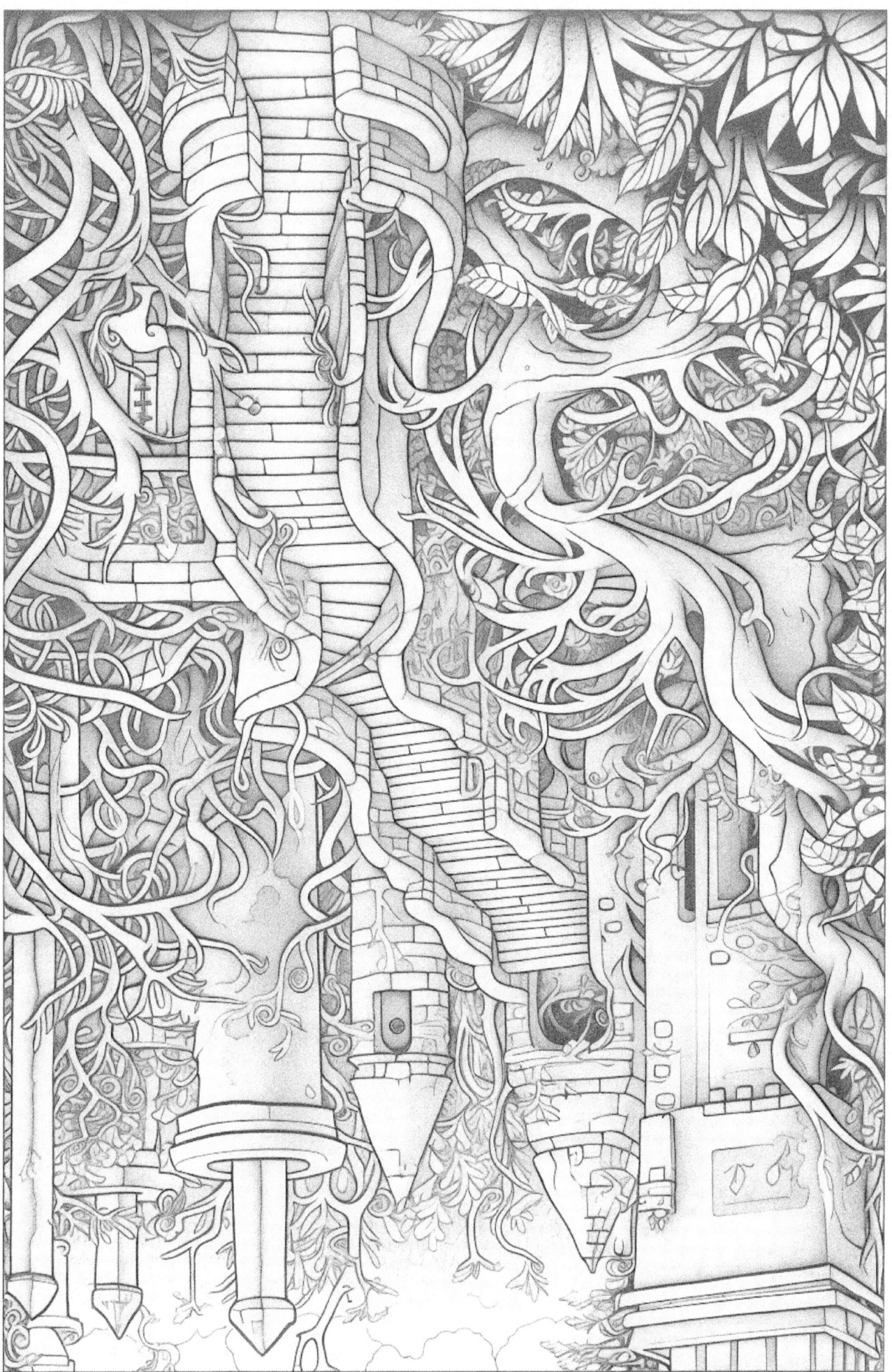

Fairies left this blank for you

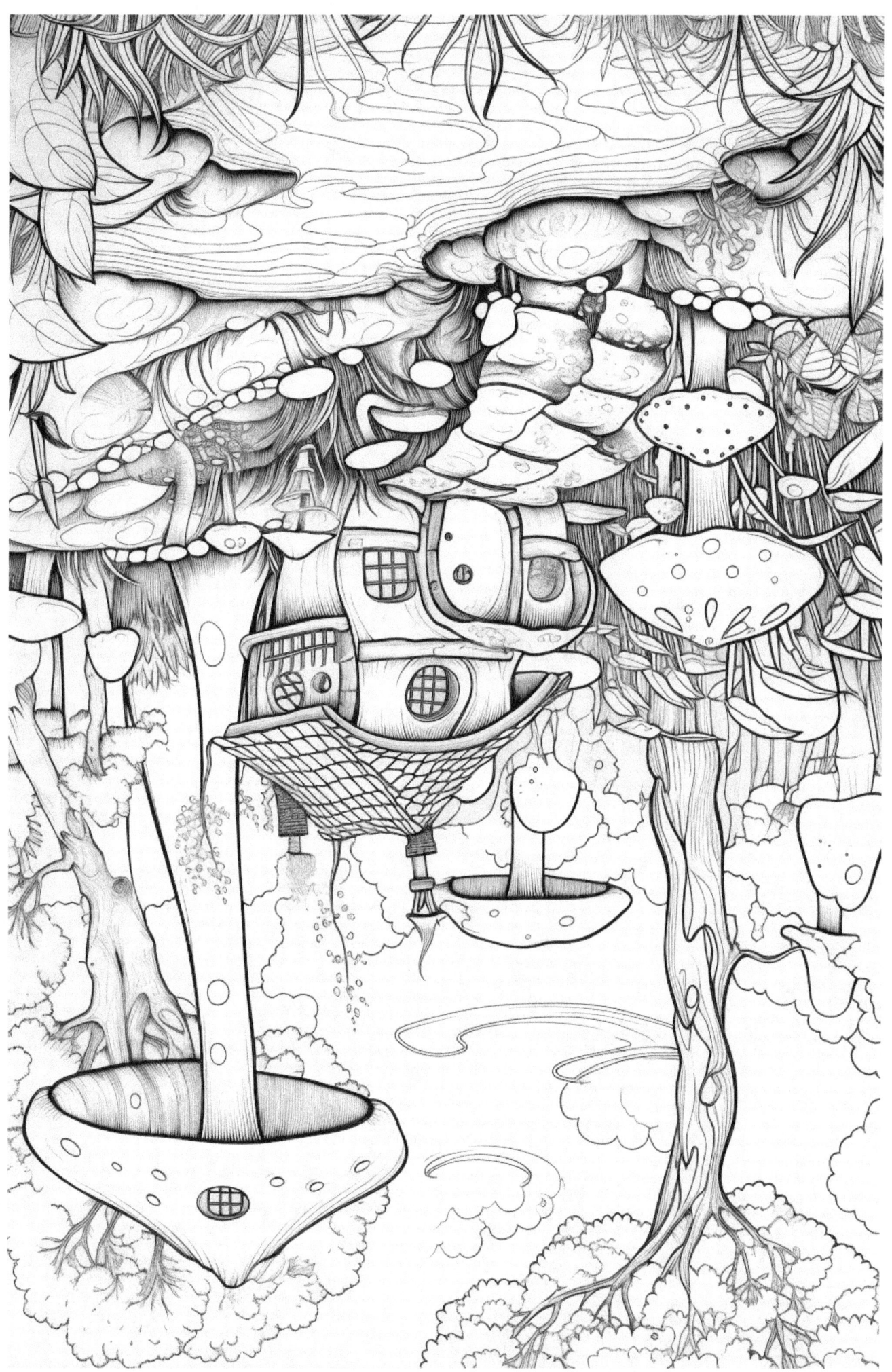

Fairies left this blank for you

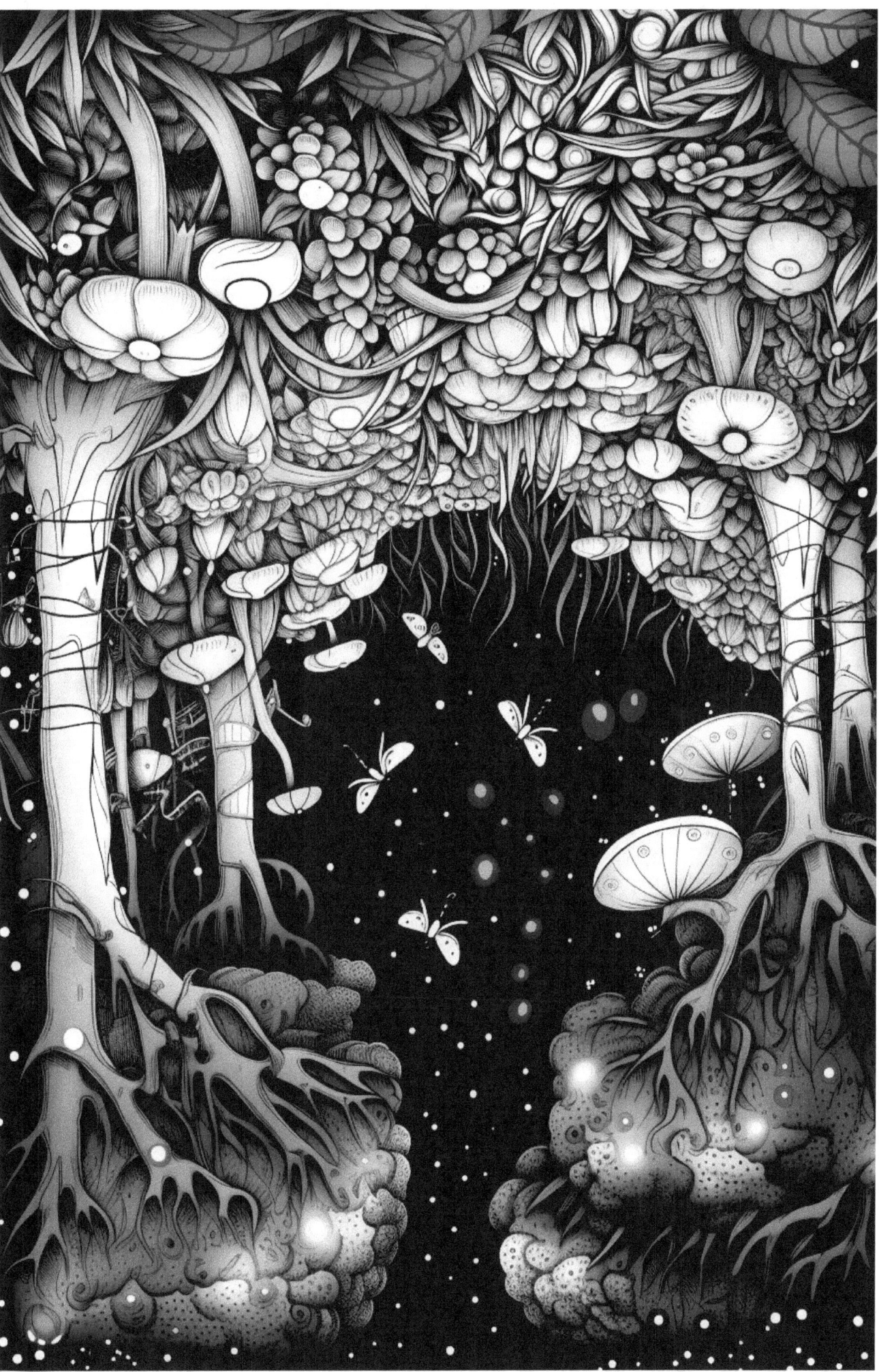

Fairies left this blank for you

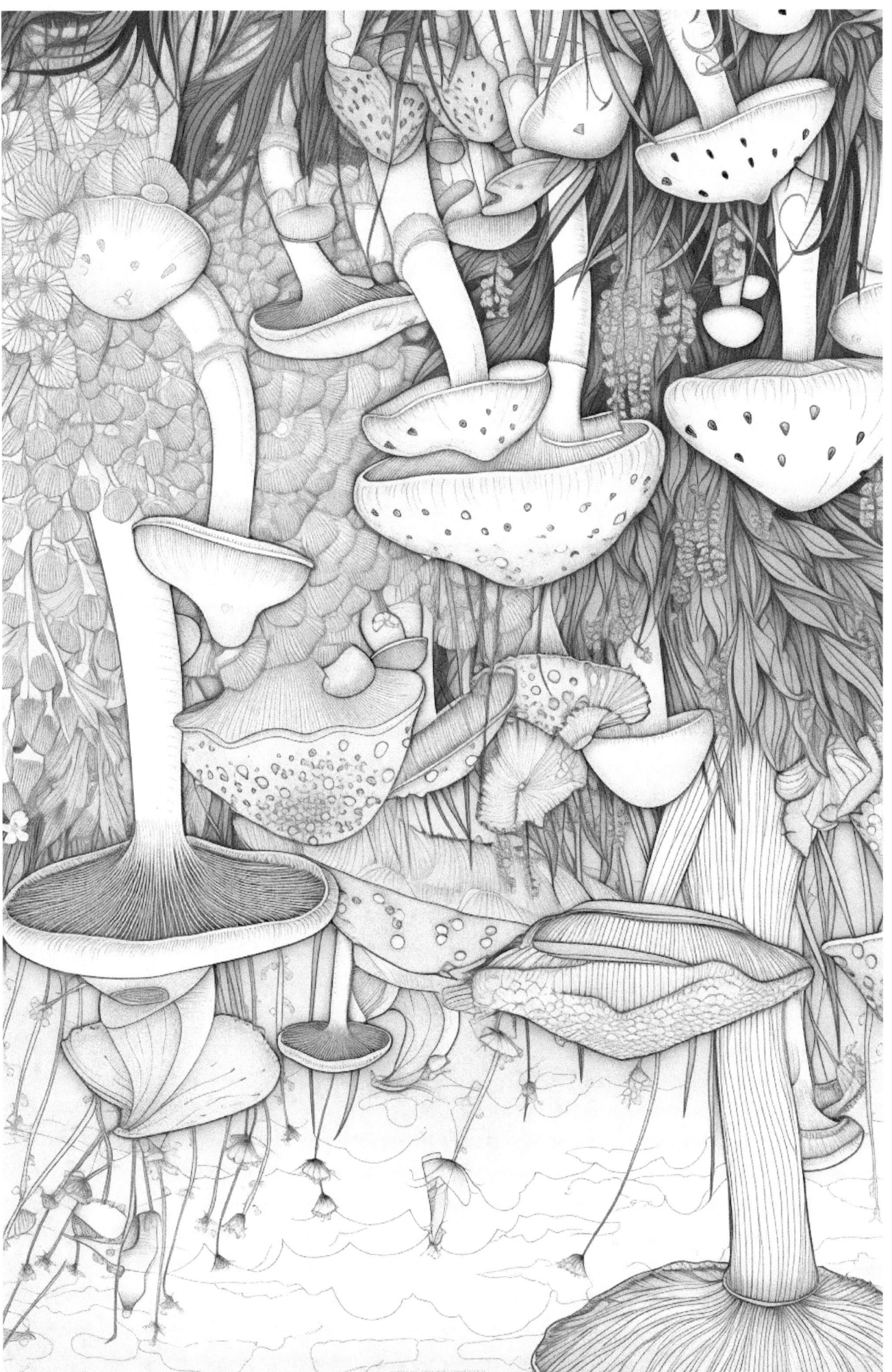

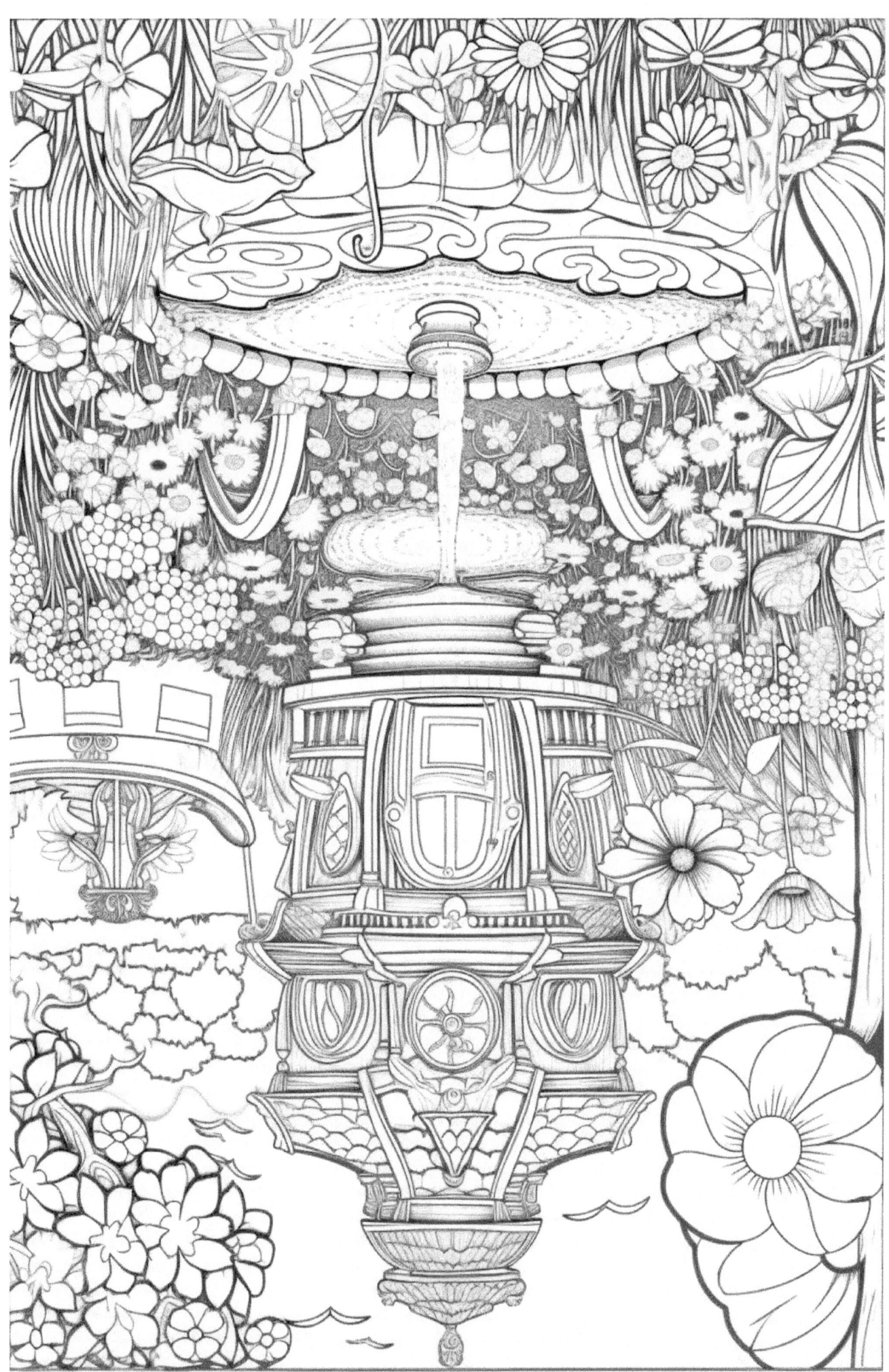

Fairies left this blank for you

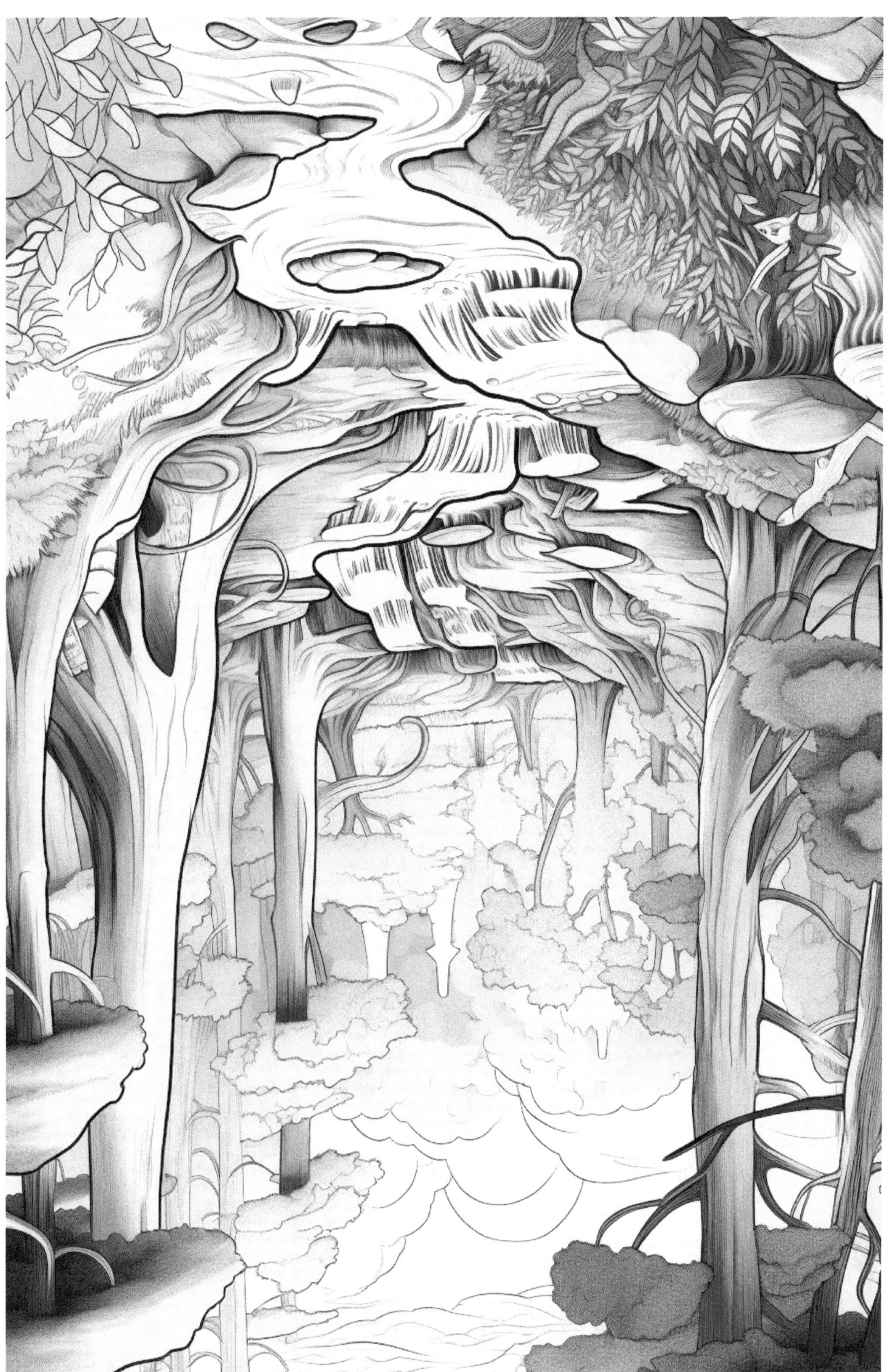

Fairies left this blank for you

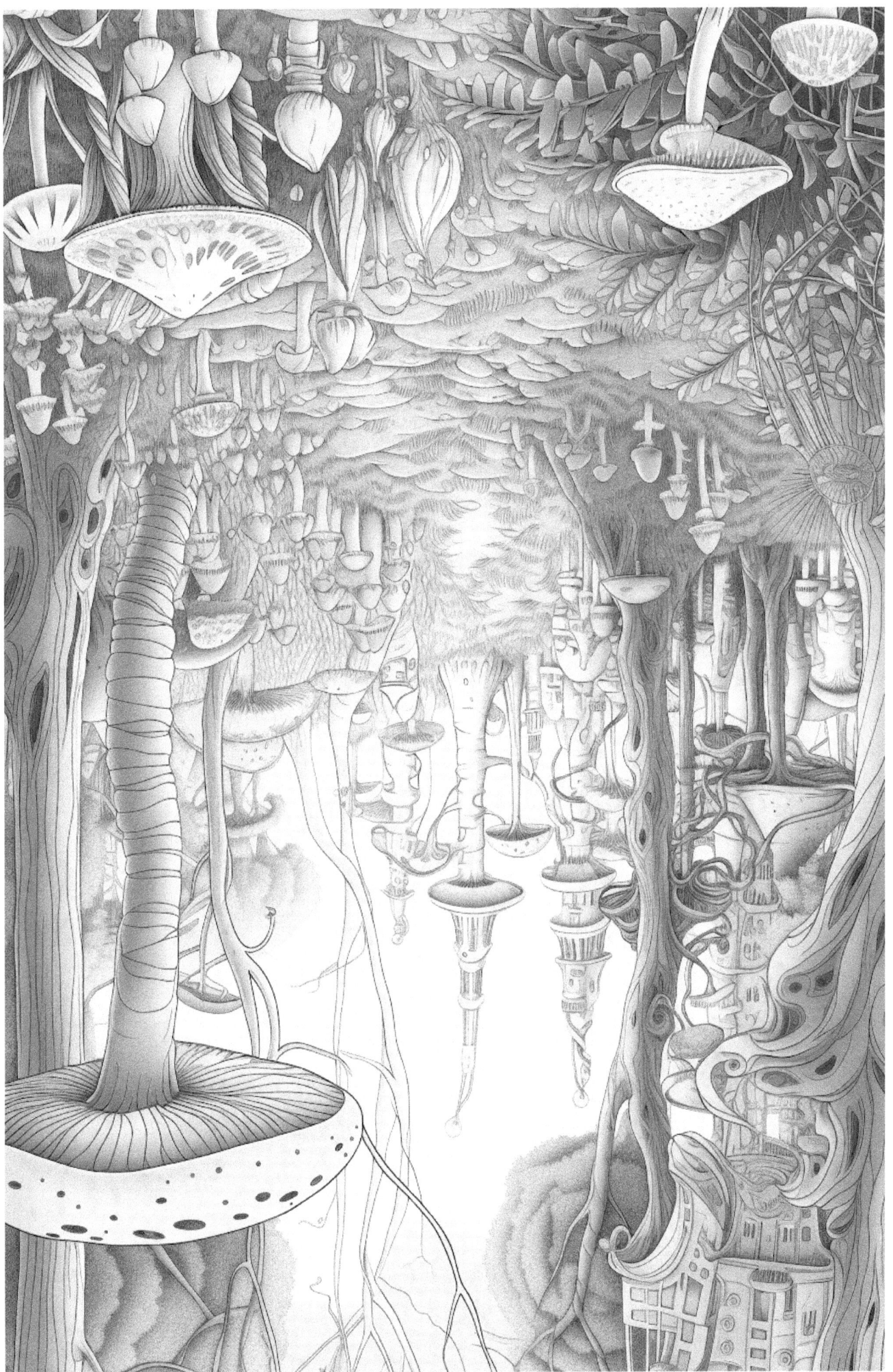

Fairies left this blank for you

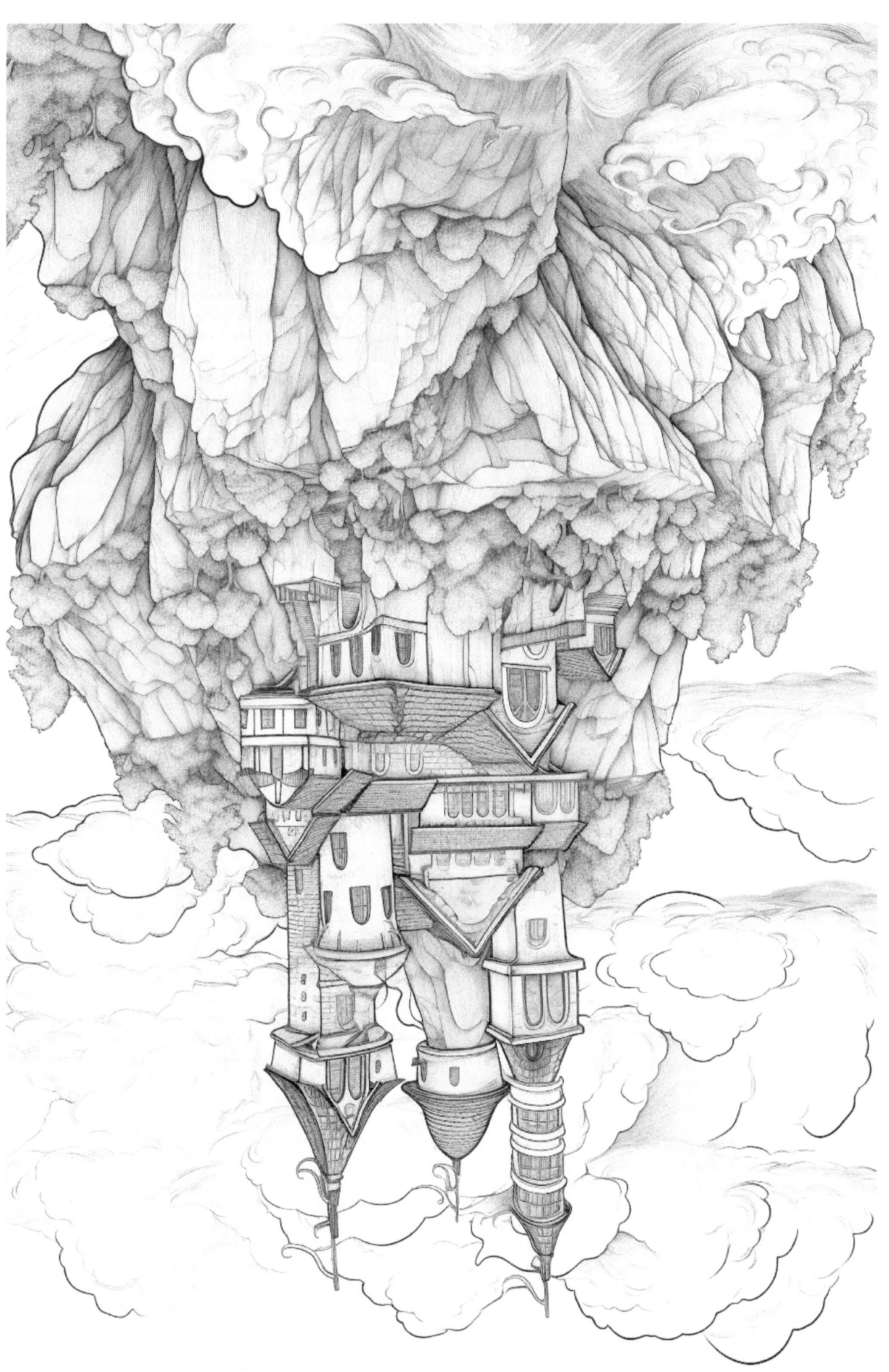

Fairies left this blank for you

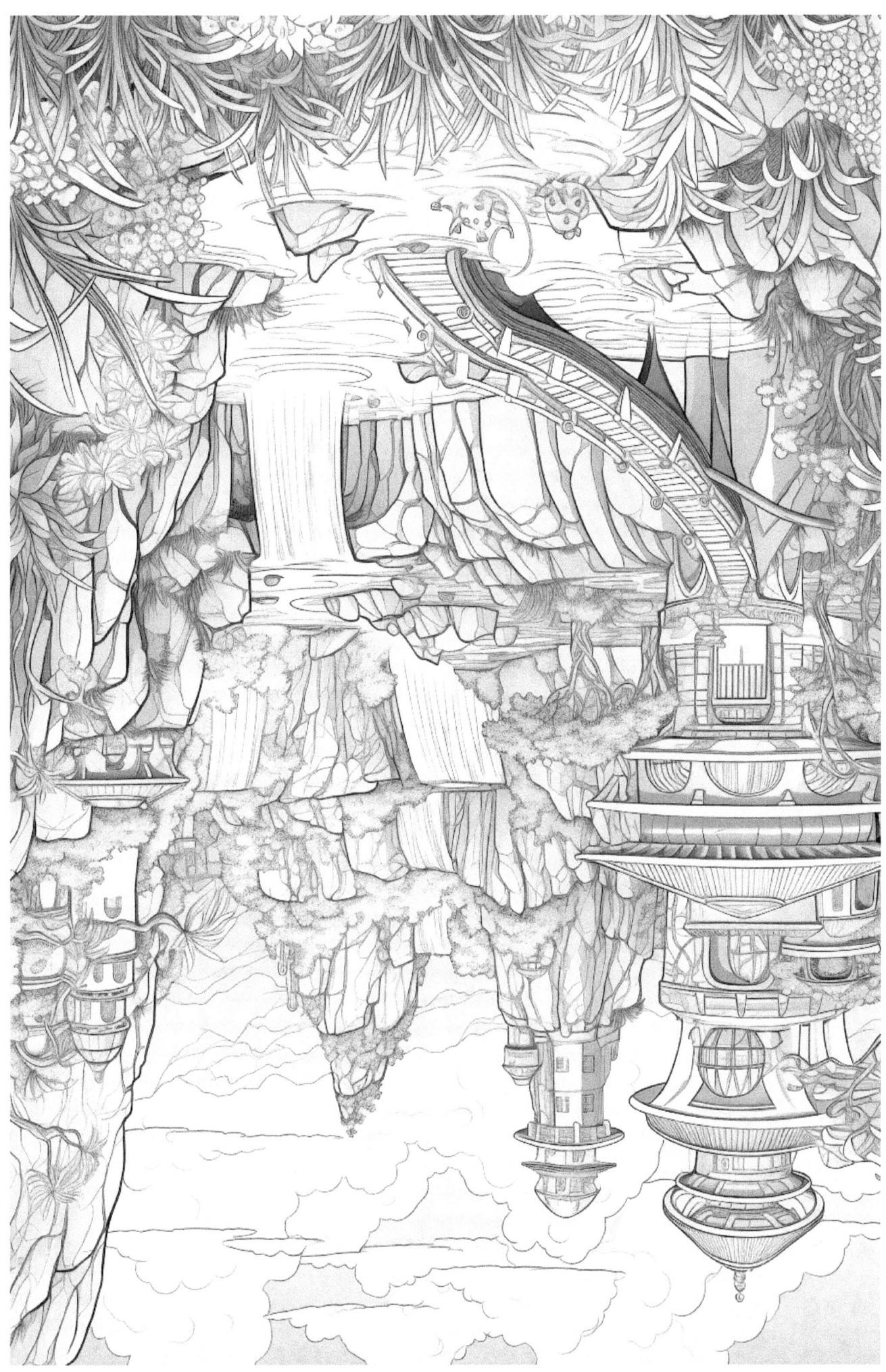

Fairies left this blank for you

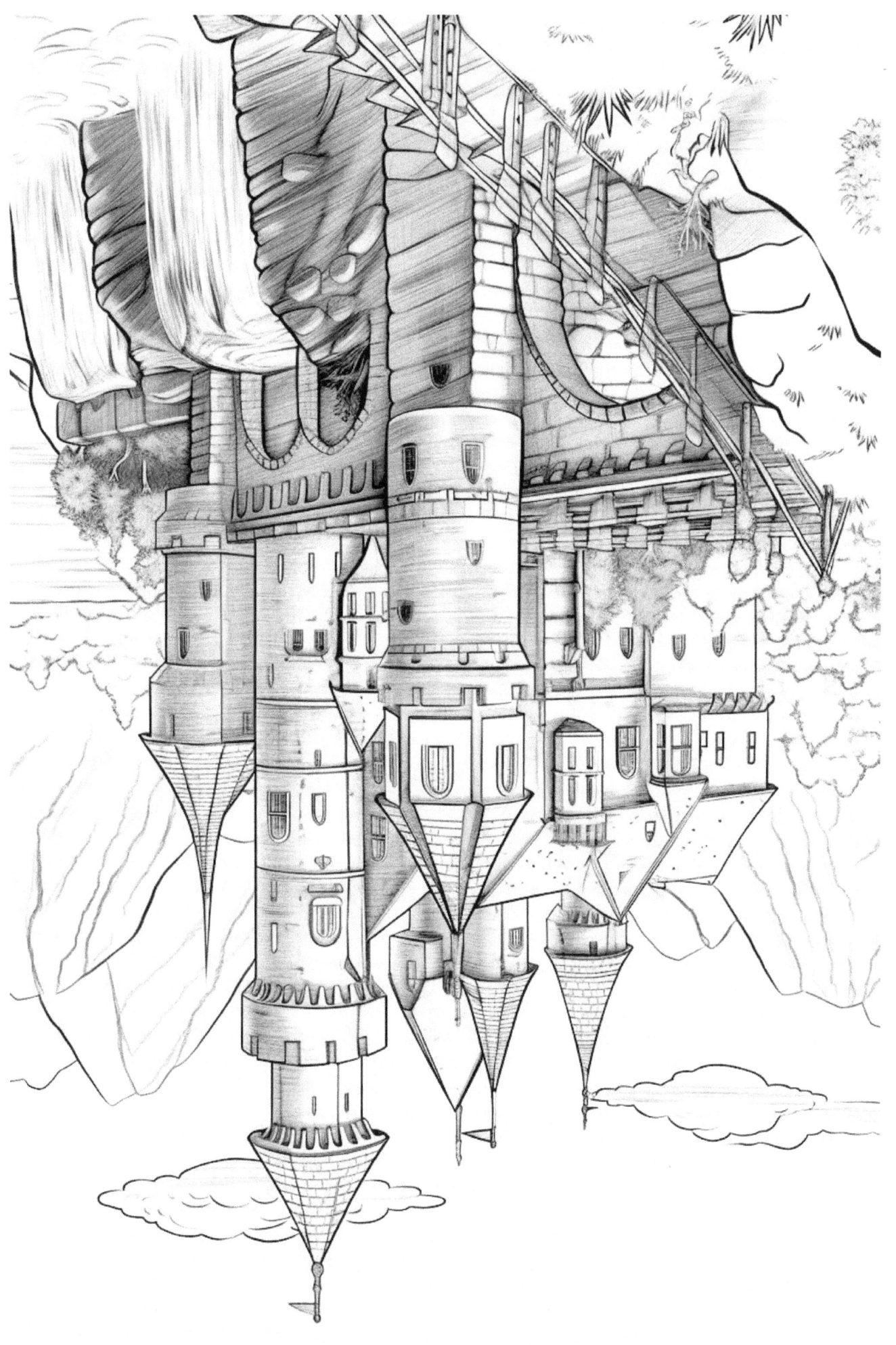

Fairies left this blank for you

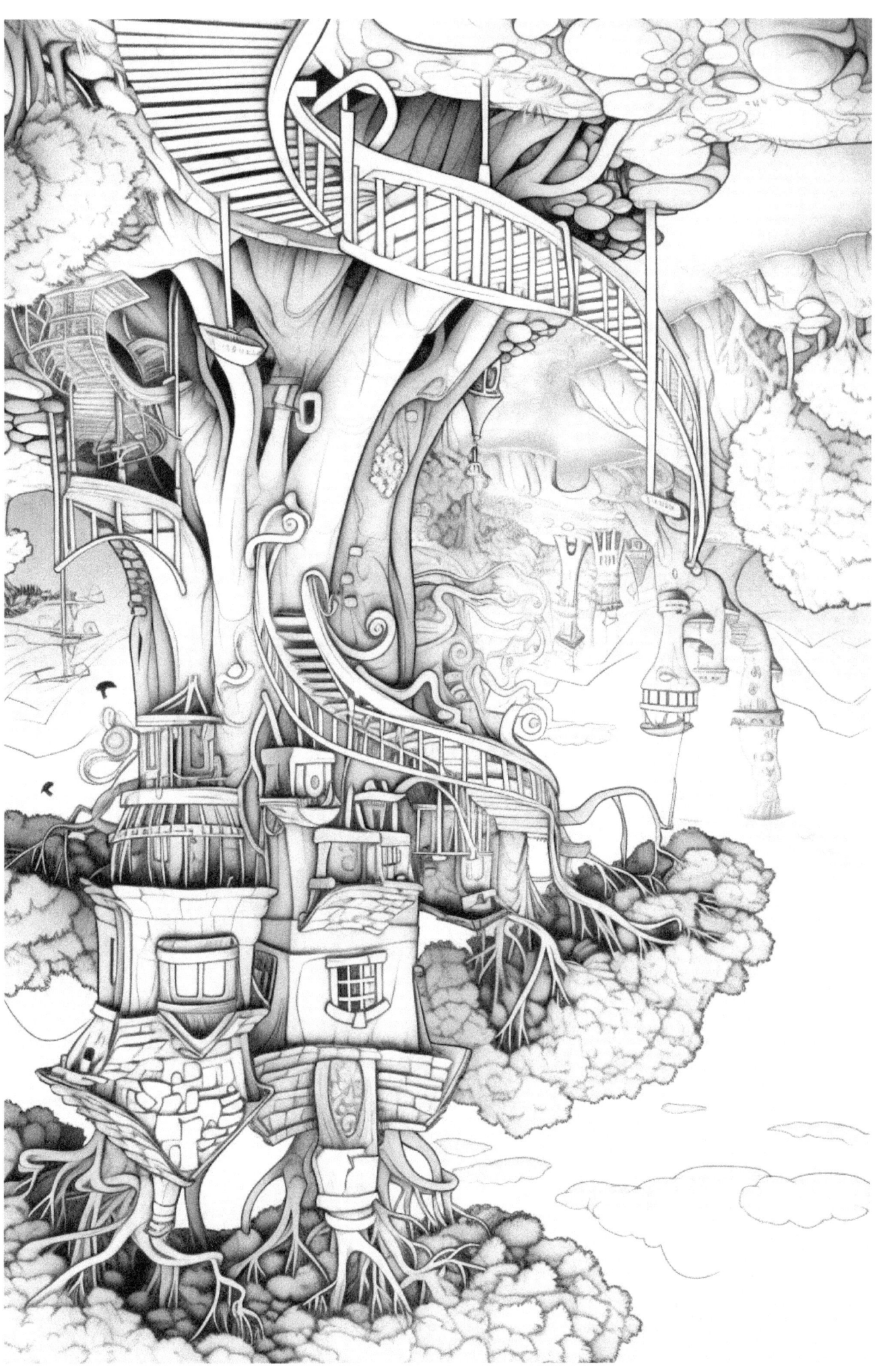

Fairies left this blank for you

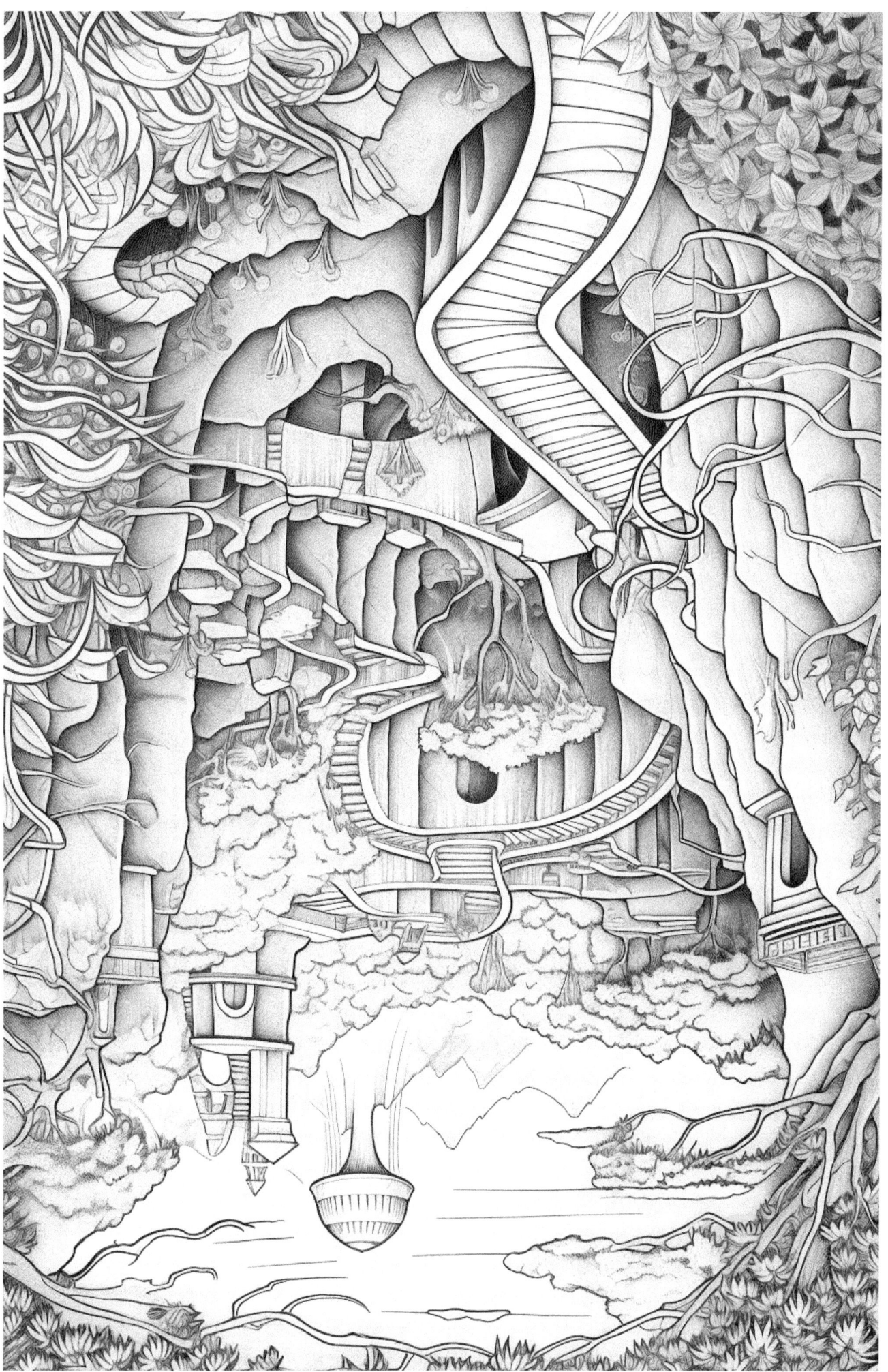

Fairies left this blank for you

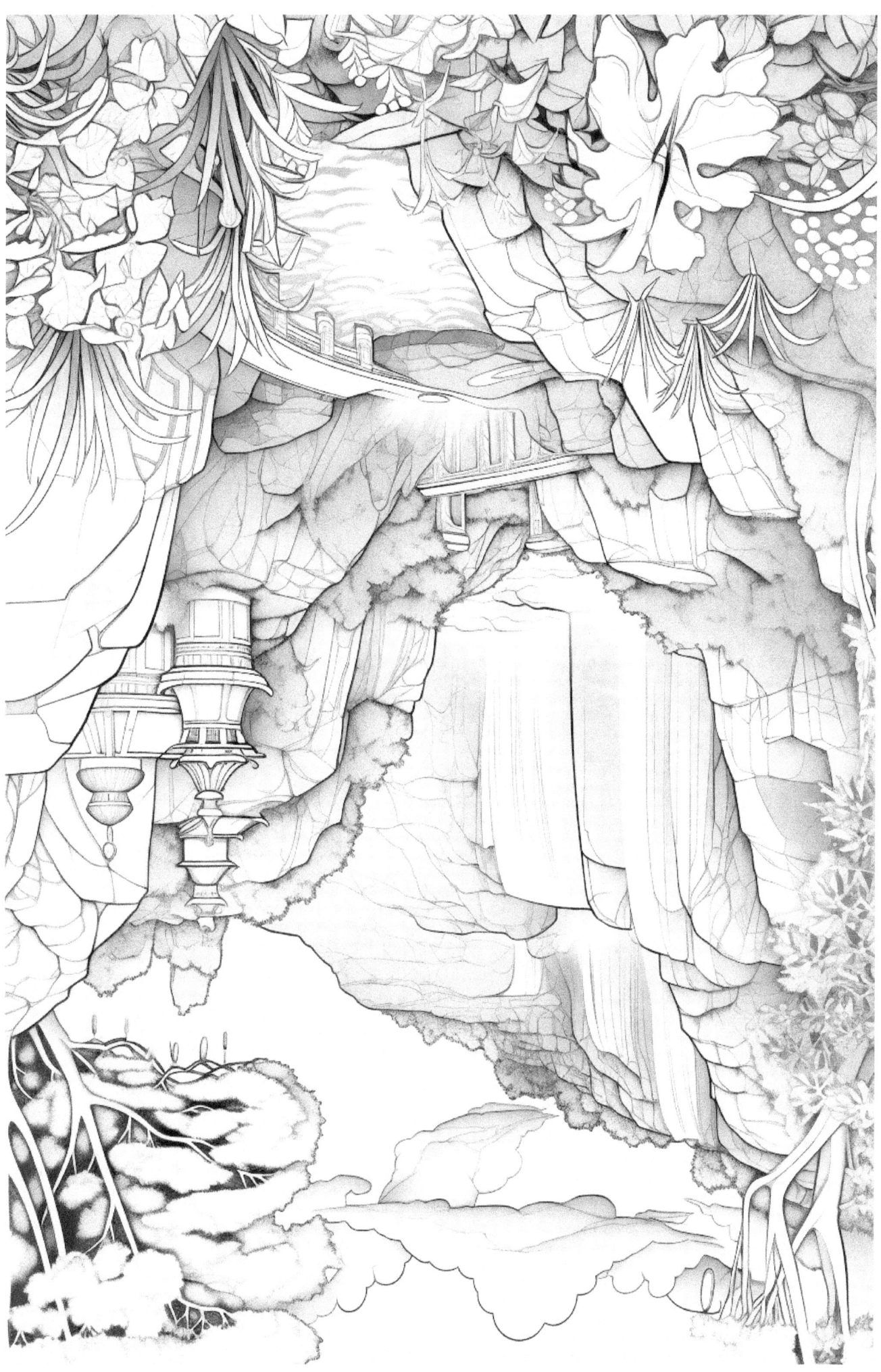

Fairies left this blank for you

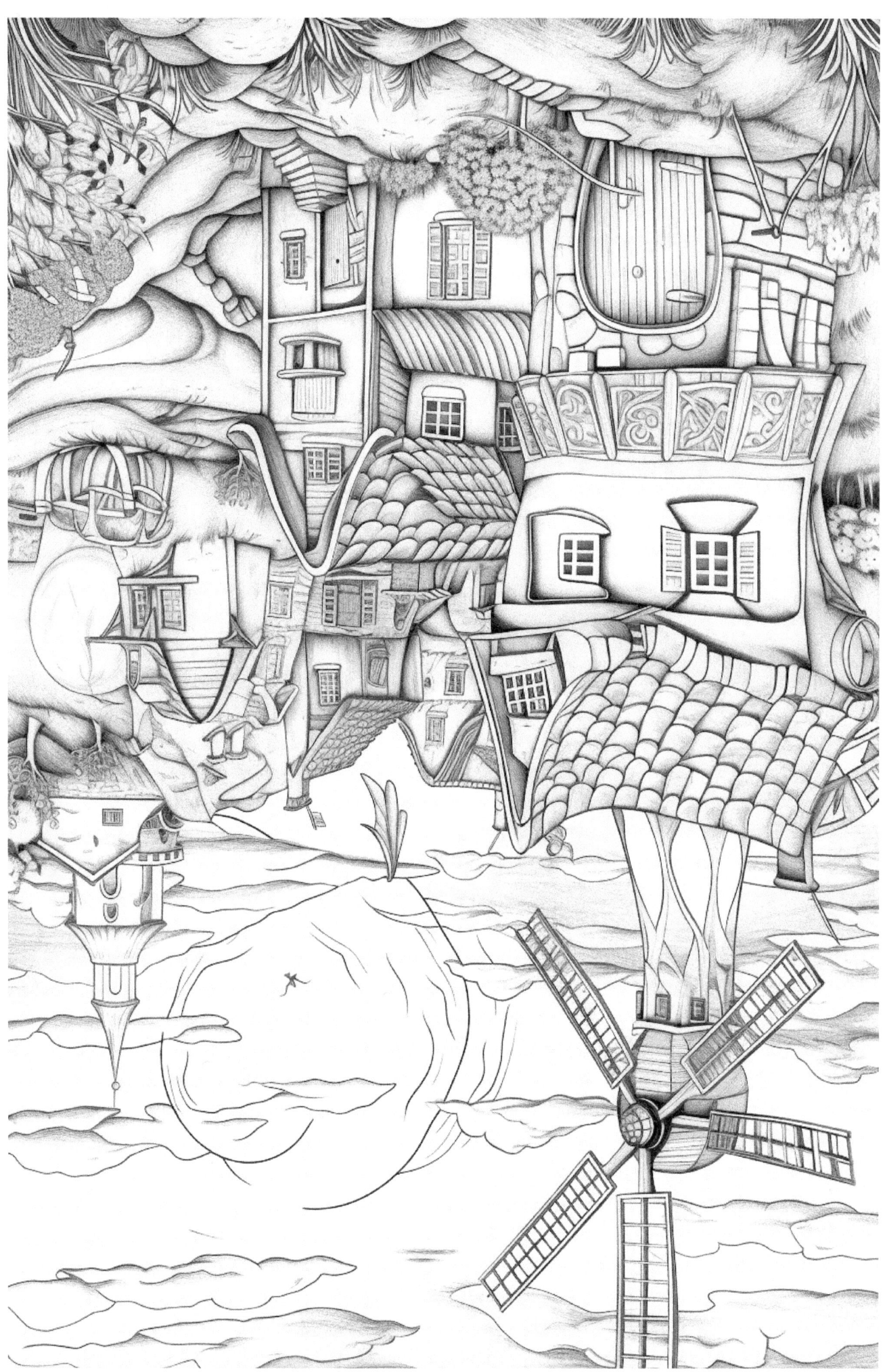

Fairies left this blank for you

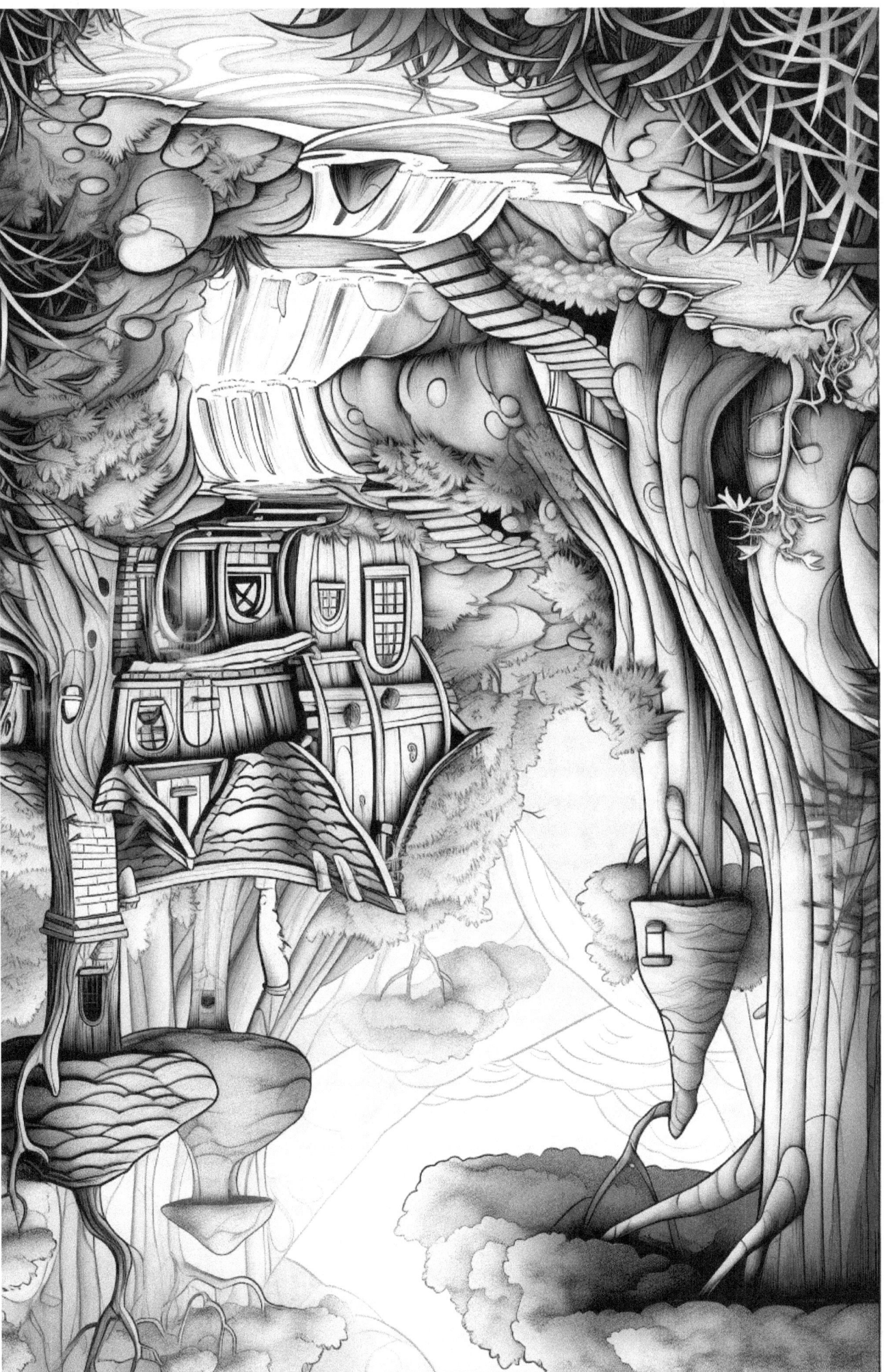

We hope you had as much fun coloring in the pages, as we had creating them!

If so, please let us and others know by leaving a review on Amazon :-)

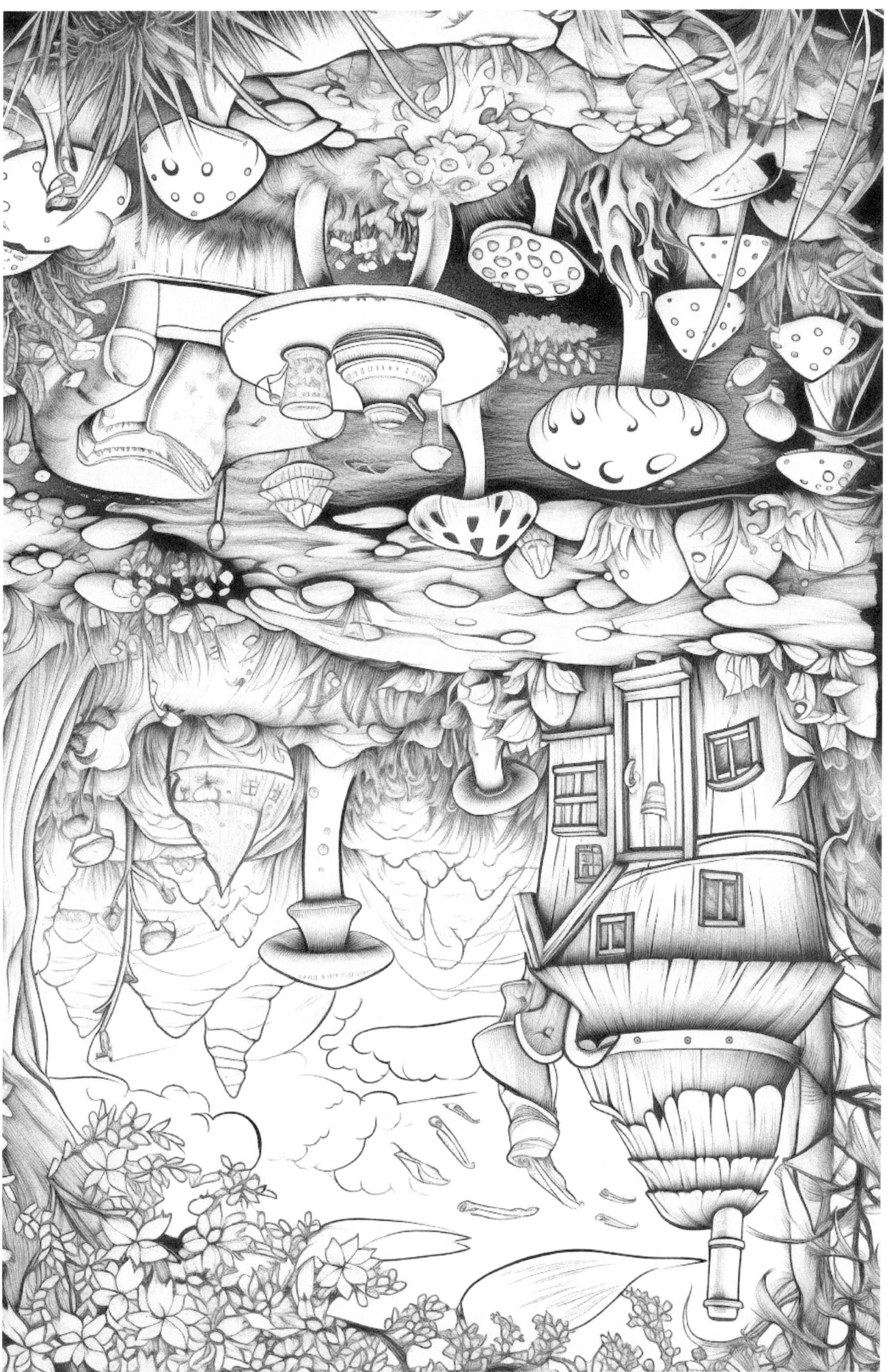